This Space; Your Place

Finding Your Path To Purpose

Gbenga Lawal

Copyright © 2024 by Gbenga Lawal

Editing, cover and author services by Opulent Books

www.OpulentBooks.net

ISBN Hardback: 978-1-916691-29-2

ISBN Paperback: 978-1-916691-28-5

All rights reserved.

No part of this publication may be reproduced, distributed, or transmitted in any form or by any means, including photocopying, recording, or other electronic or mechanical methods, without the prior written permission of the publisher, except as permitted by copyright law. For permission requests, please contact the author.

VIDEO SUMMARY

Want a video summary of this book to help you start making progress quickly? Please visit:

www.skillsmindset.com/tsyp

Dedication

To all the souls bravely journeying through life's path, seeking the thread of their unique purpose: May you find the courage to question, the strength to persevere, and the wisdom to recognise your true path when it unfolds before you. This book is a guide on your quest, a roadmap for your journey.

Remember, the search itself is as valuable as the destination.

Table of Contents

Chapter 1:	Relevance and Significance	13
Chapter 2:	Discovering Who You Are	29
Chapter 3:	Unleashing Your Gift	49
Chapter 4:	Your Gift And Leadership	67
Chapter 5:	The Importance Of Purpose	85
Chapter 6:	Discovering Your Place	97
Chapter 7:	Making Your Place Matter	111
Chapter 8:	Overcoming Barriers to Fulfilling Your Purpose	141
Chapter 9:	The Role of Success and Fulfilment In Your Life	173
Chapter 10:	Turning Challenges Into Opportunities	189
Chapter 11:	The Importance of Starting Afresh	207

Introduction

"Your work is going to fill a large part of your life, and the only way to be truly satisfied is to do what you believe is great work. And the only way to do great work is to love what you do. If you haven't found it yet, keep looking. Don't settle. As with all matters of the heart, you'll know when you find it."

Steve Jobs

In the bustling streets of our youth, amid the familiar hum of family chatter and the chime of church bells, many of us were shaped by a singular narrative: study hard, land a good job, earn well, and live contentedly. It was the same song I heard growing up, a comforting lullaby of stability and predictability. But as the years passed, a different melody began to play in the background of my life, urging me to find my unique rhythm.

I grew up in an environment where the blueprint for life was simple; School, church and work. These were the pillars of existence. Yet even in my formative years, during secondary school, a curiosity began to stir within me. I observed my friends, each one different from the next, each pursuing varied passions. There was a purity in those days; a time when competition wasn't the driving force. We simply appreciated our differences and cheered each other on.

However, as I transitioned into university, the world around me began to shift. Peer pressures mounted, and questions about life choices became more frequent and pointed. But even amidst this cacophony, a revelation dawned upon me: I had a distinct path, a purpose that wasn't defined by societal expectations. There were things I knew weren't for me, regardless of how they were

Introduction

presented. This wasn't about testing waters to see where I fit. It was a deeper recognition that some waters weren't meant for me.

A consistent thread in my life has been the desire to guide, mediate, and bring clarity to those around me. In school, they might have labelled someone like me a 'diplomat'. But as I matured, I recognised this inclination as my calling. After my National Youth Service Corps in Nigeria, a rite of passage for many young Nigerians, I embarked on a Master's programme in International Law and Diplomacy. It wasn't just about academic pursuit; it was a quest to harness my natural inclination to connect, mediate, and foster purposeful living.

Interestingly, if you had met me years ago, you'd have labelled me 'quiet'. I was the boy who would see impending danger and hesitate to voice a warning. But beneath that reserved exterior was a reservoir of thoughts, observations, and a burning desire to bring change. Over time, the urge to make a difference became so overpowering that I had to break free from my self-imposed silence.

Today, I have found *my place* in *this space*! I find joy in teaching, inspiring, and guiding people to understand that life isn't a competition. It's about recognising our unique lanes and running our races with purpose and passion. Whether leading in the Church, lecturing at a university, or consulting in leadership and skills development, I've found my arena. And now, with this book, I aim to share the lessons, experiences, and insights I've garnered over the years, hoping that they might illuminate your path to finding *your place*.

Why have I chosen to write about such a profound subject as finding one's place in the vast space of life?

Over time, I've come to realise that each of us perceives life through the unique lens of our experiences, education, and ideologies. While I've been fortunate enough to traverse varied landscapes, meet diverse individuals, and absorb a myriad of perspectives, one truth has become increasingly clear: life doesn't offer a one-size-fits-all answer.

Instead of getting lost in the vastness of life's mysteries, I believe the key lies in introspection. When we turn our gaze inwards, life begins to take on a richer hue. Understanding oneself becomes the compass by which we navigate the complexities of existence. After all, if we can't understand our essence, how can we hope to grasp the enormity of life?

It's been said that nothing in life happens without reason. Even

Introduction

when we're faced with events that defy our comprehension, events that seem random or even cruel, there's a deeper narrative at play. While we may not always discern the reasons, their existence is undeniable. This leads me to a conviction: just as events don't occur in isolation, we, as humans, aren't mere accidents in the tapestry of time. We're here with purpose, with intent.

Throughout history, mankind has been the driving force behind transformations, evolutions, and creations. If the world around us bears the mark of human touch, doesn't that signify our innate ability to shape and define our surroundings? In essence, while we are products of creation, we are also endowed with the gift of creation.

This book is an invitation to embark on a journey of self-discovery, to find that unique place where your purpose resides. It's a call to shape life, not just be shaped by it.

In *This Space; Your Place*, the term 'Space' symbolises the vast world around us which is the environment in which we find ourselves, whether by choice or circumstance. It's the backdrop against which we live our lives, filled with external influences, societal norms, and expectations. On the other hand, 'Place' signifies something deeply personal: your unique purpose and calling in this vast expanse. It's where you truly belong, where your passions and strengths converge. Throughout this book, we'll delve deeper into understanding this 'Place', helping you navigate your 'Space' to find where you genuinely fit.

Life, as most of us come to understand, isn't about what's handed to us, but rather what we make of it. This book aims to guide you through that very philosophy. Throughout my journey, I've been fortunate to immerse myself in diverse experiences, to read, to observe, and to learn. And amidst this plethora of perspectives, one truth emerged: life's essence isn't found in external definitions but in how we perceive and shape it from within.

Consider the marvels of human ingenuity. When we desire transportation, we don't merely wish it into existence. Instead, we harness the materials given to us by nature to craft automobiles. These materials didn't appear by chance; they exist for a purpose. Just as we utilise what's around us to create what we need, our existence too serves a grander design.

Every creation, be it a towering skyscraper or a piece of art, starts with a purpose and the raw materials at hand. Similarly, every individual is endowed with unique gifts and talents. We're not moulded from a singular template. Like the diverse trees in a forest, each serving a different purpose, we too have distinct roles to play.

It's easy to get caught in the whirlwind of life's complexities, to feel lost amidst its vastness. But the core of our existence lies in understanding our unique purpose. Once we grasp this, life begins to make sense. Challenges, confusions, and frustrations often stem from a lack of self-awareness. The moment we recognise our essence and our purpose, life's puzzles start fitting together.

What sets this book apart from the sea of self-help and purpose-driven narratives available today?

The journey of life is akin to navigating through an expansive forest. Some of us are born at the edge, with a clear view of our surroundings, while others find themselves deep within, surrounded by towering trees of circumstance, culture, and upbringing. Regardless of where you start, the objective remains the same: to find your path, your purpose, your 'Place' in this vast 'Space'.

Throughout the ages, countless books have been written, urging people to find their purpose, akin to telling a hungry man to eat. But what should he eat? When should he eat? Such is the conundrum of purpose. Many resources tell us to live our purpose but fall short in guiding us on how to discern, embrace, and actualise it. This book aims to fill that void.

This Space; Your Place is not just another book about finding purpose. It's a manual, a mentor, guiding you from the point of "I am here" to "This is why I am here." It offers practical insights, challenging you to move from mere existence to a life of significance. For life isn't just about birth and death; it's about the moments, choices, and actions in between - that proverbial dash between the years of our birth and death.

Every individual's journey is unique, coloured by layers of experiences and influences. However, the underlying quest remains the same: to understand oneself and one's purpose in the grand scheme of life. This book aims to be your compass in that journey, ensuring that when you look back, you can confidently say you lived a life of purpose, a life well-lived.

Discovering Meaning at Every Stage

Every human being, at some point in their journey, grapples with existential questions: "Why am I here? What is my purpose?" For some, the complex array of existence brings joy; for others, it becomes a labyrinth they never asked to navigate. The allure of

Introduction

this book lies in its universality. Whether you're struggling with life's intricacies or walking confidently on your path, this book serves as a light.

The first group this book speaks to are those drowning in life's confusion. If you've found yourself questioning the very essence of your existence or bemoaning the circumstances of your birth, this book is your compass. It says, "While you might not have chosen your start, you can choose your journey and destination."

The second group comprises those who move through life with enthusiasm but without direction. They embrace life wholeheartedly, but often find themselves lost, moving from one venture to the next without a clear sense of purpose. To them, this book provides a map.

Then there are those who, despite being ensconced in their purpose, may feel a need for reaffirmation or a desire to help others find their path. To these seasoned travellers, this book offers insights and challenges.

History is replete with tales of late bloomers like Colonel Sanders of KFC, who found profound purpose post-retirement. It's testament to the fact that it's never too late to find or redefine your purpose. Age is but a number when it comes to living a life of significance.

The essence isn't about the length of our lives but the depth. We're called not merely to exist but to make a mark, to contribute in ways both big and small. This isn't solely a Christian philosophy; it's a universal truth. The very devices and innovations we use daily, from our smartphones to our cars, were birthed from someone's purpose. They're a testament to human potential and innovation.

So, what then is your legacy? What footprint will you leave behind? *This Space; Your Place* isn't just another idea; it's an invitation to a journey of self-discovery and significance, urging every reader to not just live, but to live well and with purpose.

No Matter Where You Are In Life, This Book Will Help You

As we stand on the brink of a journey through the chapters of *This Space; Your Place*, I'd like you to envision this book as satellite navigator. No matter where you are in the trajectory of your life, whether at the budding dawn of youth or the golden afternoons of latter years, the understanding and realisation of purpose is ageless and timeless.

Introduction

In the forthcoming chapters, we will go deeply into the realms of relevance and significance, exploring their intricate dance and how one doesn't necessarily translate to the other. We will embark on the most crucial journey of all – the journey inward. The voyage of self-discovery is one that unveils the treasure of our unique gifts, the beacon that illuminates our path to leadership and purpose.

As you navigate these pages, you'll be offered tools and strategies to overcome barriers, turn challenges into stepping stones, and redefine success in a way that resonates with true fulfilment. You'll be inspired by stories of those who, against all odds, found their purpose or started anew, reminding us that every moment is ripe with potential.

I implore you to approach this read with an open heart and an eager mind. Let the wisdom within these chapters serve as a guide, prompting introspection and sparking a flame of purpose that has perhaps dimmed or has yet to be ignited.

As we prepare to turn the page to Chapter 1, remember that this isn't just a book – it's an invitation. An invitation to understand deeper, to search further, and to live with a passion that radiates from the core of your very being. I promise, by the end, you won't just be standing in *'This Space'* but firmly rooted in *'Your Place'*. Let the journey begin.

Chapter 1

❝

Relevance and Significance: Understanding the Difference

❞

"One of the huge mistakes people make is that they try to force an interest on themselves. You don't choose your passions; your passions choose you." **Jeff Bezos**

This Space; Your Place

The memory of my first job is still as vivid as the colours of a fresh painting. I remember walking into that office, the excitement of a new chapter mixed with the trepidation of unknown challenges. The role seemed clear-cut, and to the world outside, I was on a path that many would envy. But deep inside, there was an inkling, a whisper, hinting that perhaps this wasn't the entirety of my journey.

In those early days, my job was about databases. On the surface, it might seem like a world of cold numbers and faceless data. However, the essence of my role was about people – understanding their needs, habits, and patterns. But there was a gap between the kind of connection I was fostering in my job and the depth of connection I yearned for in my heart.

It's a sentiment many echo. Across the globe, countless individuals wake up every day, following routines they've established over years, even decades. Yet, when they pause, often during the twilight of their careers, a realisation dawns. There's a voice inside, a persistent hum, declaring there's more to life, more to give, more to experience.

Consider the many stories of those who, after a lifetime in a chosen profession, pivot dramatically. Medical professionals turning to farming or charity, bankers finding solace in teaching, and engineers tapping into their latent artistic passions. Their transitions aren't driven by financial motives but by a profound quest for significance, a longing to align with a deeper purpose.

Your purpose is the central motivating aim of your life. It's not just a fleeting thought or a whimsical wish; it's a compelling force. Purpose shapes our goals, influences our actions, and gives meaning to our days. It's like an internal compass, guiding us through life's untold decisions, big and small.

Jesus Christ, in His profound wisdom, once remarked, "My food is to do the will of Him who sent me and to finish His work." This sentiment underscores the essence of purpose. It's not just about starting; it's about completion, fulfilment, and resonance.

Defining Relevance

Our birthright isn't just about relevance; it's about leaving an indelible mark of substance. Let's pause for a moment and discover what relevance truly means.

At its core, relevance is about occupying a position of importance in a particular context or space. It's about fame, position, affluence, power, authority, and possessions. It's the throne you sit on, the brilliance you exude, and the riches you accumulate. These attributes, while valuable, serve as the external markers of one's standing in society. They are essential for societal recognition, for establishing relationships, and for navigating the complex tapestry of human interactions.

Reflect upon the various leaders and authority figures we encounter in our lives. There are individuals in traditional roles who, despite mixed opinions about their leadership style or decisions, occupy key positions. Whether it's a prime minister, president, or head of state, these figures exemplify relevance in their domains. They might not be universally liked or revered, but their roles are undeniable and essential for the functioning of society.

Here's the key insight: relevance isn't just about the position you hold; it's about understanding and acknowledging the weight of responsibility that comes with it. It's about recognising that you are needed, that you hold value, and that you have a part to play in the larger narrative. It's a delicate balance of supply and demand, of identifying needs and fulfilling them, of recognising problems and providing solutions.

As we journey through life, seeking to understand our purpose and place, relevance becomes the stepping stone. It positions us in the right direction, aligning us with the tasks we are meant to undertake. It's the initial recognition that we matter, that our contributions have value, and that we are part of a larger web of interconnected lives.

However, while relevance is crucial, it's just the beginning. As we'll explore in subsequent chapters, moving from relevance to significance is where the real journey begins. It's about transcending the external markers of success and tapping into the deeper, more profound essence of purpose and contribution. But for now, let's embrace the notion of relevance, understanding its importance, and recognising its place in our journey of self-discovery and purposeful living.

Defining Significance

While relevance might position us in society's spotlight, significance delves deeper, reaching into the core of our purpose and the essence of true fulfilment. To truly understand life and our place within it, we must grasp the profound distinction between being relevant and being significant.

At its core, significance is an echo of our deepest purpose, resonating with our truest sense of fulfilment. Imagine standing at the pinnacle of relevance, surrounded by the trappings of power, position, and prestige. Yet, without significance, this pinnacle can feel hollow. It's the depth of our impact, the difference we make in the lives of others, and the legacy we leave behind that defines our significance.

Reflect for a moment on the countless individuals who've reached the zenith of their professions, achieved fame, and yet, later in life, pivoted towards charitable endeavours, outreach, or other purpose-driven initiatives. Why? Because while their earlier pursuits made them relevant, they yearned for the depth and richness of significance. They sought purpose, fulfilment, and a lasting impact that extended beyond the self and resonated with the wider community.

Being significant means asking the deeper questions: "Why am I here?"; "What lasting impact can I make?"; "How can I elevate not just myself, but those around me?". It's about realising that life's true treasures aren't just in the accolades we receive, but in the lives we touch and transform.

Remember, relevance can place you on the map, but it's significance that etches your legacy into the annals of time. As we navigate the journey of life, we must constantly challenge ourselves, asking not just how we can be relevant, but how we can truly matter. It's not merely about occupying a space but about defining it with purpose and passion.

For many of us, our journey's early phases might be driven by the pursuit of relevance. But as we mature, evolve, and reflect, the quest for significance takes centre stage. And it's in this quest that we find our truest calling, our most genuine self, and our most profound sense of purpose.

From Business Mogul to Children's Champion

The life journey of Charles Mutua Mulli is inspiring. In his earlier years, Mulli faced immense hardships, including abandonment by his family. Yet, he overcame these adversities and went on to establish a successful business, amassing considerable wealth and becoming a notable figure in his community. This status epitomised relevance. Mulli's success in business and his standing in society were undeniable.

As time progressed, Mulli felt a deeper calling towards significance. Inspired by a series of personal encounters and reflections, he made the profound decision to sell his businesses and dedicate his life to the service of vulnerable children. In 1989, he founded the Mully Children's Family (MCF), a charitable organisation that has since provided home, education, and vocational training for thousands of street children and orphans in Kenya.

Charles Mutua Mulli, once primarily known as a successful businessman, is now also recognised as a champion for children in need. His journey from relevance (through his business achievements) to significance (through his charitable efforts with MCF) is powerful evidence of the distinction between the two concepts. While his business successes positioned him in the limelight, it's his tireless efforts to uplift and empower vulnerable children that will cement his legacy of significance.

Mulli's story exemplifies the journey from achieving personal success and relevance to seeking broader significance by making a profound impact on society. We are born not only for relevance but for significance.

Popularity and Significance: Not Always Equal

In the age of social media, viral videos with millions of views have become a common phenomenon. Often, these videos are

Relevance and Significance

mere clickbait, designed to lure us in with tantalising titles or thumbnails. While they might momentarily captivate our attention, they seldom leave a lasting impact. Yes, they are popular and relevant for a fleeting moment, but do they hold any real significance? The answer is typically 'no'.

Many conflate the idea of popularity or fame with significance, but these are distinctly separate concepts. Popularity is about being known, being in the limelight, and often, being momentarily relevant. Significance, on the other hand, delves deeper. It's about the lasting impact one makes, the value one brings, and the legacy one leaves behind.

Imagine preparing a meal. In the midst of cooking a creamy cheese pasta, you realise you're missing a crucial ingredient - cheese. The absence of cheese will profoundly affect the outcome of the dish. Similarly, in the vast recipe of life, every individual is an ingredient. Their unique value, skills, and contributions determine their relevance. However it's the depth of their impact that dictates their significance.

Just as a missing ingredient can alter a meal's outcome, a person's absence in a particular space can change the course of events. This isn't just about being present but about understanding one's unique role and contribution. It's not about merely occupying space but about understanding one's purpose within that space.

Many chase fame, position, and authority for the sake of recognition, but what do they truly achieve with their influence? It's essential to reflect upon one's motivations. Is it merely for the allure of popularity, or is there a deeper drive to bring about meaningful change?

While many can attain popularity, not all translate it into significance. As we navigate *this space*, we mustn't just focus on being relevant but also strive for true significance. We are not born merely to be popular; we are born to leave a mark of significance in this vast world.

Why Relevance Does Not Guarantee Significance

Life often presents us with dualities: light and shadow, success and failure, relevance and significance. Each has its place, and each holds a lesson. But today, we explore the fascinating dynamic between relevance and significance, exploring why the former does not guarantee the latter.

When I embarked on my professional journey, I was quickly

introduced to the concept of relevance. It was the currency of the corporate world. If you were relevant, you had a seat at the table; you had a voice that others listened to. Relevance often comes clad in the trappings of titles, accolades, and positions. It is the applause after a well-delivered presentation, the nods of approval in meetings, the recognition of being 'needed' or 'important' in a particular setting. Relevance is, in many ways, the external validation of our role in a system or structure.

But here's the caveat: relevance is transient. It's tied to circumstances, to the ever-changing dynamics of the world around us. Today's relevant expert can be tomorrow's outdated professional. Today's trend-setting influencer can be tomorrow's forgotten voice. Relevance, while valuable, is often a fleeting, surface-level measure.

This brings us to significance, the deeper, more enduring sister of relevance. Significance isn't just about having a role; it's about the depth and impact of that role. It's not just about being present; it's about making that presence truly count. Significance is the legacy we leave, the lives we touch, and the difference we make. It's about depth, purpose, and lasting impact.

A person may hold an important position in a company,

making them highly relevant. But if their actions, decisions, and leadership don't create lasting positive change or if they don't mentor and uplift those around them, is their contribution truly significant? Positions, ranks, and titles are inherently temporary, but the way you treat or influence people will always hold significant permanence.

The crux of our exploration is this: while you can be relevant without being significant, you cannot be truly significant without also being relevant. True significance, grounded in purpose and positive impact, naturally elevates one's relevance. It ensures that you're not just a fleeting name on a chart but a force of change, and a pillar of legacy.

> *Positions, ranks, and titles are inherently temporary, but the way you treat or influence people will always hold significant permanence.*

Your search for significance is about carving out *Your Place* in *This Space*. It's not just about being present but making your presence felt in a profound way. While relevance situates you within the current dialogue, significance ensures that your contributions to the conversation are remembered, cherished, and continues to inspire.

In *this space* of ever-evolving trends and shifting dynamics, it's essential to not just fit in but to stand out, to not only be a part of the story but to leave an enduring legacy. That's the difference between just occupying a space and truly owning *your place*.

Purpose is connected to significance. It's the underlying 'why' that directs our actions, decisions, and choices. In essence, understanding and immersing oneself in their purpose is a process of recognising and operating in one's unique 'place' within the vast 'space' of the universe. We will talk more about this in chapter 6.

For instance, consider Nelson Mandela. To the external world, his relevance began with his anti-apartheid activities and grew immensely during his 27 years of incarceration. He was known, respected, and even feared by some for this. But his significance goes far beyond just being an anti-apartheid revolutionary. His 'place' or purpose became evident in his unparalleled commitment to peace and reconciliation upon his release. Instead of seeking vengeance for the years lost and the injustice suffered, he championed a vision of a united South Africa, where all races lived in harmony. His purpose wasn't just to fight an oppressive system but to sow the seeds of unity and forgiveness in its aftermath.

Many can occupy a relevant position in the 'space' - be it a job title, a societal role, or a recognised status. But not all who are relevant in such ways tap into the deeper significance of their 'place' or purpose. The difference lies in the depth of impact and the legacy left behind.

Another final but critical point to note in the journey of purpose is that time and change are crucially imminent. Invest in yourself and in time, and prepare to manage the inevitable changes. Don't squander your precious time dwelling on the sorrows of your past. Look straight ahead, believe in God, and believe in yourself. Don't allow people to ridicule your struggles; you're on a significant journey. Your end has not yet come. You cannot have a better tomorrow if you're dwelling too much on yesterday. There is glory in your tomorrow.

Chapter 1 Highlights

- Relevance is the currency of the corporate and societal world, but it's fleeting. It's tied to circumstances and can change as dynamics evolve.

- Significance is about carving out your unique place in the vast space of the universe. It's about leaving a lasting legacy.

- Popularity or fame doesn't equate to significance. True significance is about the lasting impact we leave on others and the world.

- In the quest for a fulfilling life, it's essential not only to be relevant but to strive for profound significance.

Chapter 2

Discovering Who You Are

"Give out what you most want to come back." **Robin Sharma**

This Space; Your Place

Once upon a time in a sprawling meadow, a donkey, with dreams in his eyes, decided to build a house. He envisioned a simple, comfortable abode tailored to his needs. As he began laying the foundation, a passing rabbit, with a twinkle in its eye, remarked, "Why not add a burrow underneath, like mine? It's a brilliant way to stay cool in the summer."

Desiring to accommodate the rabbit's advice, the donkey incorporated a burrow.

Next, an ostrich, fluttering its large wings, suggested, "Imagine a high perch where you could gaze upon the horizon. It's breath-taking from a height, even if it's not as high as the sky!"

Once again, eager to take on board the ostrich's idea, the donkey added a perch to his design.

Soon after, a frog, its skin glistening under the sun, hopped by and commented, "Your house is taking shape nicely, but you ought to add a pond. There's nothing like a refreshing dip to rejuvenate oneself."

The donkey, increasingly unsure of his original vision but not wanting to disappoint, added a pond.

As days turned into weeks, many animals of the meadow

offered their unique suggestions. The donkey, with a heart keen to please, incorporated all their ideas. By the end, his house was an amalgamation of burrows, perches, ponds, webbed corners, and other features that stood in stark contrast to one another.

One day, a wise old tortoise, with years of wisdom etched on its shell, ambled by and remarked, "Whose eclectic house is this?"

The donkey, with a hint of pride, replied, "It's mine."

The tortoise, gazing thoughtfully at the house and then at the donkey, mused, "But does this house truly represent you, or is it a mirror reflecting everyone else?"

The donkey paused, the weight of the tortoise's words sinking in. He realised that in his quest to accommodate everyone's suggestions, he had lost sight of his own identity and desires.

Following the tale of the donkey, it becomes evident that one's identity can easily be swayed by the myriad voices and opinions surrounding us. Falling into the trap of conforming to others' expectations or attempting to fit into prescribed moulds can lead to a loss of one's true self.

You can't be constantly swayed by every passing trend or suggestion. If you do, you'll find yourself in a perpetual race to meet others' expectations. When you are constantly reacting to external prompts, you're essentially allowing others to dictate your path. They say, "Do this," and you comply. Another voice chimes in, "Now try that," and you heed. This lack of grounding can lead to feelings of being lost, being everywhere and yet nowhere at all.

It's not about mindlessly emulating others, especially when their path or style doesn't align with your core values. Blindly copying or trying to be someone you're not can result in missteps. You might find yourself in unsuitable environments, associating with groups or organisations that don't resonate with your beliefs. Such misalignments can lead to dissatisfaction and even distress.

Understanding and embracing your identity is paramount. To truly know who you are, you must delve deep, reflecting on your values, passions, and aspirations. You need to clearly define your identity for yourself, setting boundaries and understanding what truly resonates with your soul.

That's why a satellite navigation system in your vehicle or mobile device is useless without you entering a destination because it lacks direction and purpose. Without a clear understanding of one's identity, values, or goals, the path forward becomes uncertain and ambiguous.

Discovering Who You Are

An undefined journey leads to no destination. When you embark on a journey without a defined sense of self or purpose, it becomes challenging to make decisions that align with your true desires. This lack of clarity can result in feelings of confusion, indecision, and a constant state of searching without finding fulfillment.

Moreover, without a defined destination, measuring progress or success becomes difficult. A well-defined destination acts as a guiding star, providing motivation and focus along the way. It allows for the setting of milestones and goals, enabling one to track progress and make adjustments as needed to stay on the right path.

Remember, while it's beneficial to seek inspiration and learn from others, it's equally crucial to stay true to oneself. It doesn't matter the number of people running beside you; make sure you stay in your own lane. In a world full of voices, make sure you listen to the one that matters most: your own.

> *It doesn't matter the number of people running beside you; make sure you stay in your own lane. In a world full of voices, make sure you listen to the one that matters most: your own.*

The Quest for Identity

The question of identity is profound and enduring. Throughout history, humankind has grappled with this enigma, seeking to understand who we are at our core. The issue of stolen, lost, or obscured identity has been a recurring theme in literature, philosophy, and psychology. Will we ever find exhaustive answers to this profound question? The search might be endless, but it's a journey worth embarking upon.

Unravelling the layers of one's identity requires introspection. It compels us to question our beliefs, motivations, and actions. Who are you, truly, beneath the roles, titles, and masks? Where do you stand in the grand tapestry of existence? Why do you make the choices you do? The answers lie within, waiting to be discovered. This journey of self-discovery, of digging deep into one's psyche to unearth one's true essence, is transformative.

As the esteemed Dr. Myles Munroe often highlighted in his speeches and books that there are two pivotal moments in a person's life. The first is the day of their birth, marking their entrance into this vast world. The second, and perhaps even more profound, is the day they discern the 'why' behind their existence. It's the day they recognise their purpose, their unique contribution to the world.

While many might pass through life without grasping the depth of their significance, the moment of self-realisation is transformative. It's akin to a rebirth. Suddenly, the world seems different; perspectives shift, priorities realign, and a newfound clarity emerges. The day you truly discover yourself, your purpose, is, I believe, the day your authentic journey begins. It's the day you break free from external constraints and begin to chart your own path, guided by an internal compass that points towards your true worth.

The Importance of Self-Discovery

The journey of self-discovery is a pivotal one, a voyage that goes deep into the essence of one's being. To genuinely comprehend who you are, it's imperative to understand and define your identity. This quest for identity goes beyond surface-level attributes. While factors like gender can play a role in shaping our identity, the true essence of self-discovery lies in understanding the core of our being.

The identity in question here isn't just about external markers. It's not solely about gender, though that can play a part. It's about unearthing the genuine self beneath societal expectations, roles, and facades. Throughout history, there have been countless tales of individuals undergoing profound transformations upon discovering their true selves. Some have felt so transformed by this revelation that they've chosen to change their names, symbolising a rebirth of sorts. Others have relocated, seeking environments more conducive to their authentic selves. Many have even made drastic career changes, realising that their previous vocations were misaligned with their true passions.

Furthermore, self-discovery often leads to a re-evaluation of personal habits and choices. Some might abandon certain habits, not due to societal pressure, but because of a deep-seated understanding of what's beneficial for them. They might recognise that certain substances or behaviours adversely affect them, and, armed with this knowledge, choose a different path. Even if everyone around them indulges in a particular activity, those who've truly discovered themselves can confidently decline, standing firm in their self-awareness.

For instance, one of my business partners is lactose intolerant. Despite the allure of creamy desserts and cheese-laden dishes at business dinners and gatherings, he steadfastly avoids anything containing lactose. He knows all too well the adverse reactions he faces when he consumes such items. It's not about resisting temptation or adhering to dietary trends; it's a matter of understanding and honouring his body's needs. No matter how tantalising a dish might look, his decision to abstain is rooted in self-awareness and the importance of prioritising his well-being. Not every good thing is necessarily good for you.

The journey of self-discovery is about discerning the difference between who the world thinks you are and who you truly are at your core. It's about stripping away the layers of societal expectations and peer pressures to reveal the authentic self beneath. And in that unveiling lies the power to live a life of genuine purpose, passion, and fulfilment.

One of the business tycoons who profoundly inspires me is Sir Richard Branson, founder of the Virgin Group. His story is not just about entrepreneurial exploits, but it's also harnessing the power of self-discovery.

Facing the challenges of dyslexia, Branson could have been confined by the boundaries of traditional education and societal norms. Yet, he charted his own path, driven by a deep understanding of his strengths and passions. Leaving school at 16 to pursue his entrepreneurial dreams might have seemed unconventional to many, but for Branson, it was a reflection of his self-awareness.

His journey from a basement magazine start-up to a global business empire underscores the importance of recognising one's inner truths and acting on them. Each of Branson's ventures, be it in music, aviation, or space travel, reflects not just his business acumen but his commitment to staying authentic to himself.

In a world that often prescribes fixed paths and benchmarks for success, he exemplifies that when we align our actions with our personal truths, we can achieve unparalleled success.

Sir Richard Branson's story resonates deeply with me, reminding me of the limitless possibilities that arise when we truly understand ourselves and have the courage to act on that knowledge.

Your self-discovery is the beginning of your self-expression. Imagine taking a fish out of water and placing it on land alongside other animals. As a farmer, you might have many creatures in your care, but placing a fish among them on dry land would be strange. The fish wouldn't thrive, not because it lacks value or purpose, but simply because it's in an environment where it cannot truly express itself. Just as the fish is ill-suited to life outside of water, individuals can feel out of place when they are not in settings that resonate with their true selves. It's not about the fish being redundant; it's about recognising the importance of the right environment for authentic expression.

Everything has its rightful place in this world. Each entity, each being, has a specific environment in which it thrives best. As individuals, it's paramount for us to discern two fundamental truths: firstly, recognising the unique 'species' or category to which we belong, and secondly, understanding the environment in which we can best express and fulfil our potential.

For example, spirits cannot function in our world without inhabiting a body. This realm, with its distinct characteristics, necessitates a physical form for interaction and expression. Similarly, one wouldn't venture to the moon in everyday attire; the environment there demands specialised equipment to ensure survival and functionality.

Drawing a parallel to our own lives, it becomes evident that self-discovery is not just a luxury, but a necessity. To truly thrive, to genuinely make a mark, people must first understand who they are at their core. Only then can they discern their purpose, recognising not just what they wish to achieve, but also where and how they should pursue those aspirations.

Practical Steps to Self-Discovery

1. Consult the Creator

One fundamental step towards understanding oneself is seeking insights from our origin – our Creator. Just as every invention bears the blueprint of its maker, every individual carries within them a purpose set by their Creator.

For many, including myself, the most straightforward path to self-discovery is by reconnecting with our Creator. Think about it: if you purchase a gadget, it often comes with a manual from the manufacturer, detailing its functionalities, capabilities, and best practices. This manual is a direct insight into the creator's intent for the gadget. Similarly, by turning to the source of our existence, we can gain clarity about our purpose and potential.

When we fail to consult this 'manual' or remain disconnected from the Creator of *this space*, we might misuse our innate abilities and potential. Just as a device can be damaged or become inefficient when not used according to its manual, so too can we become less effective, or even harm ourselves, when we act contrary to our true nature.

It's the manufacturer who defines a product's purpose and potential. If the purpose of an item isn't understood, it leads to misuse or even abuse. Similarly, if we don't comprehend our true purpose, we run the risk of misusing our talents, leading to feelings of frustration, resentment, and dissatisfaction.

King Solomon, one of history's wealthiest and wisest rulers, provides a compelling example of the profound impact of seeking guidance from our Creator.

Solomon, upon ascending to the throne of Israel, was presented with a unique opportunity in a dream. Solomon, despite being a king with vast resources at his disposal, recognised the significance of wisdom from his Creator. He understood that true prosperity and success come not just from material wealth, but from aligning oneself with higher principles and seeking purpose and understanding from the Creator.

A clear indicator of whether you're aligned with your purpose is to gauge your emotions. Are you frequently angry, envious, or caught up in unhealthy competition? While competition and comparison have their places, especially if they serve as motivation and checks on one's progress, they can be detrimental when misplaced. For instance, comparing a marathon runner's performance to a sprinter's is illogical. They have different training regimes, tracks, and end- goals.

> *If you find yourself constantly looking over your shoulder, measuring your progress against someone on a completely different path, it might be an indication that you're not on the right track for yourself.*

If you find yourself constantly looking over your shoulder, measuring your progress against someone on a completely different path, it might be an indication that you're not on the right track for yourself.

2. Identify Your Passions

Often, the things we are truly passionate about can provide significant insights into our purpose and identity. Start by asking yourself: what activities or subjects ignite a fire within you? What tasks or hobbies do you find yourself lost in, where hours feel like minutes? These passions, these burdens of the heart, often hold clues to our true calling.

For instance, if you find yourself consistently drawn to stories of social injustices and feel a deep-seated urge to make a difference, perhaps you're meant for a career in activism or social work. On the other hand, if the intricacies of the digital world fascinate you, maybe you're destined for a role in technology or digital innovation.

Once you've identified these passions, it's crucial to test them in real-world scenarios. Engage in activities or pursue courses related to your interests. This hands-on experience will either solidify your passion or help you realise that perhaps it was more of a fleeting interest rather than a lifelong calling.

Take, for example, the story of a close colleague of mine. From his earliest memories, he has been fascinated with books. Reading them, writing them, even the mere presence of books seemed to energise him. Every week, without fail, he'd add to his ever-growing collection. This wasn't just a hobby; it was a passion. As time went on, his fervour for literature not only remained steadfast but evolved. What he hadn't realised in those younger years was that this passion would one day morph into a thriving business.

Today, he aids aspiring authors in bringing their visions to life, guiding them in writing and publishing their works. His venture started from a place of passion, and by identifying and nurturing it, he's now facilitating others, including myself, in realising their dream of becoming published authors.

3. What Problems Can You Solve?

Every individual in *this space* is intricately woven with the potential to make a positive impact, to serve, and to be the answer to a specific problem. So, what are the challenges that resonate with you? What issues tug at your heartstrings and push you to act?

Consider the medical profession. A trained and qualified medical doctor, upon entering a hospital, is immediately recognised and acknowledged for his role. His very presence signals healing, care, and expertise. That's the essence of identifying your calling. When you step onto your platform or field, those around should instinctively sense, "Ah, here's the solution we've been waiting for."

Your journey of self-discovery should lead you to that unique space where you're not just existing but illuminating the path for others. It's about emerging from the shadows, shining brightly, and moving forward with purpose, ensuring that your presence translates to solutions, guidance, and answers for those in need.

Tesla, Inc., spearheaded by Elon Musk, serves as a prime example of identifying and solving a significant global challenge, subsequently generating profit through innovative solutions. Musk pinpointed the issue of heavy reliance on non-renewable energy sources for transportation, which contributed to environmental degradation and climate change. In response, Tesla developed high-performance electric vehicles and renewable energy products, aiming to shift global reliance on fossil fuels towards a sustainable energy future. In this venture, Musk identified a significant problem, came up with an innovative solution, and, through his company, generated profit while aiming to provide long term benefits to society.

As you embark on this journey of self-discovery, it's not only essential to identify and embrace your calling but also to understand the rules and principles governing your chosen path. Just as every environment has its distinct protocol, every passion or career has its own set of guidelines, norms, and ethics.

Once you've discerned your purpose and can visualise the work you're meant to do, it becomes paramount to acquaint yourself with the rules of that realm. It's akin to learning a new game; how can you possibly play, let alone excel, if you're unaware of its rules?

Every sphere of life, be it professional or personal, is governed by a set of natural, societal, or divine principles. These principles serve as the backbone of that domain, ensuring order and structure. Without a grasp on these foundational rules, one risks feeling lost, overwhelmed, or even inadvertently causing harm.

Furthermore, it's vital to recognise that everyone's journey is distinct. While some may require five tools to achieve their goals, others might need just two. It's detrimental to compare your journey to another's, as such comparisons can lead to frustration, envy, and even an abrupt end to your own unique path.

Understanding oneself is the cornerstone of leading a life steeped in purpose. Knowing who you are, recognising your strengths, acknowledging your weaknesses, and discerning your passions are paramount. It's not simply about recognising your identity; it's about deeply comprehending your essence and the intricate nuances that make you unique.

The Bible highlights that while all things may be permissible, not all are beneficial. This sentiment underscores the importance of discerning choice. Just because one can do something doesn't necessarily mean one should. Your true calling may require you to forgo certain pleasures or activities not because they are inherently wrong, but because they don't align with your purpose.

Your identity influences every facet of your life, from the friendships you cultivate, the environments you thrive in, to the foods you consume. It serves as your moral compass, guiding your decisions, big or small.

Consider the idea of reputation and legacy. When people mention your name, what comes to their mind? Ideally, it should be synonymous with your purpose, your passion, and your contributions to the world. This clarity is achieved only when one is in tune with their inner self.

Sadly, in today's world, many grapple with the challenge of self-identity. It's not uncommon to witness individuals oscillate between different personas, trying to fit into various moulds. Such fluctuations often stem from a lack of self-awareness, leading to frustration and confusion. When I was younger, I too grappled with understanding my true self. It's a journey, one that often requires introspection and sometimes even a retreat from the chaos of daily life. Communing with the Creator, reflecting on one's life and realigning with one's purpose is a pivotal step in this journey of self-discovery.

Chapter 2 Highlights

- Practical steps for self-discovery include consulting the Creator, identifying passions, and recognising unique problems one can address.

- Comparing individual journeys can be detrimental as your race is different from the next person.

- Personal identity plays a pivotal role in life choices and influences one's reputation and legacy.

- Many struggle with self-identity, but introspection and reconnection with one's purpose can provide clarity.

Chapter 3

Unleashing Your Gift

"If you don't define your direction, you will end up in no destination." **Gbenga Lawal**

This Space; Your Place

Do you know that everyone has gifts in *this space*? No one is born empty handed. Yes the Creator endowed us with multiple gifts. Not just one but many. The beauty of our gifts, much like the heritage of a plant garden, is that they continue to grow, to evolve, and to surprise us. You might think you are familiar with the contours of your abilities, but there are depths yet to be plumbed, facets still unpolished. Life has a way of presenting us with stages upon which to perform, challenges that call forth gifts we never knew we possessed.

At the heart of this book lies a fundamental truth that I wish to convey to you. Every individual born into this world is here for a purpose, and to navigate this purpose, he or she is endowed with essential tools. These tools manifest as what we call our 'gifts.'

Consider for a moment that life is akin to a mission, a quest you've been tasked with. Just as a skilled artisan is provided with a set of instruments to craft a masterpiece, so too are you equipped with a unique set of talents and abilities to accomplish your life's work. These gifts are intrinsic; they are the very mechanisms by which we can fulfil our designated roles.

It's crucial to grasp that these gifts are not of our own making.

We did not sit at the drafting table when our life's blueprint was being drawn up. Our purpose was not our choice, nor were we conscious participants in its conception. It is a path laid out for us – a path we must endeavour to discover as we journey through life.

The gifts we possess are akin to a compass pointing us towards our destiny. They are the silent allies that energise us, enable us, and empower us to make a meaningful impact. It is through the realisation and application of these inherent gifts that we find the ability to be of service not just to ourselves but also to those we are meant to reach.

In essence, what I'm articulating is that while we may seek to understand the 'why' of our existence, it is the 'how' that is often illuminated by our gifts. We are vessels of potential, charged with purpose, and fuelled by the innate talents that we bear. These gifts are the keys to unlocking our contributions to the world, enabling us to leave an indelible mark in *this space*.

In our pursuit of a meaningful existence, it is essential not only to fulfil the duties of our chosen professions but also to nurture the gifts that are uniquely ours. This dual commitment to our job and our personal calling is echoed in the ancient wisdom of Ecclesiastes in the Bible, which advises us to: "Sow your seed in the morning, and at evening let your hands not be idle, for you do not know which will succeed, whether this or that, or whether both will do equally well."

This verse serves as a powerful reminder that our daily work is not the sole measure of our life's purpose. While we toil in our professional fields, there is a deeper 'work' within us that demands attention – our inherent gifts and passions. It is in the quiet cultivation of these gifts that we often find our truest joy and satisfaction. As such, I encourage my readers to invest time each day to hone and develop their innate talents. In doing so, we honour not just the responsibilities of life but also its richness and potential for personal fulfilment. Whether it is early in the morning or late in the evening, let us not allow idleness to rob us of the opportunity to grow and contribute in the most authentic ways possible.

Gifts Are Like Seeds

Imagine standing upon the precipice of discovery, where every step forward is a step into the vastness of your own potential. It's as if you have been handed a map to a treasure that lies within you, a treasure trove of abilities, each with its own unique lustre and value.

Unleashing Your Gift

Gifts are like seeds that, when nurtured, can grow beyond what you ever imagined. They can push through the toughest soil and reach for the sun. But they require you to take the steps of planting, watering, and tending to them.

> *Gifts are like seeds that, when nurtured, can grow beyond what you ever imagined. They can push through the toughest soil and reach for the sun. But they require you to take the steps of planting, watering, and tending to them.*

Your gifts, whether they roar like the engines of progress or whisper like the gentle flow of a river, are yours to share with the world. It's not merely about possessing them; it's about the courage to use them, to allow them to take flight.

I have often wondered about the gifts that I carry. I want to use my example to show you how these gifts are related and complement each other. They are dynamic. I've come to recognise the diversity of gifts that each of us harbours, often lying in wait like seeds underground, ready to spring forth with the right nurture. I have the gift of wisdom, that has often guided me and others through the fog of indecision and complexity. It is this wisdom that stands at the helm when I navigate the waters of life and work.

Yet, this gift does not sail alone. Accompanying it is what in management we refer to as strategic thinking. This capacity to foresee, to plan, to envision not just the next step, but the next hundred steps, is intrinsic to my approach, both in life's plans and its daily endeavours. It is a cornerstone of leadership – which is another gift, allowing me to steer the ship, not just with foresight but with insight. It is seeing beyond the horizon, discerning pathways where others may see dead ends.

Administration and management too are spheres where my abilities manifest. In these realms, I find my gift for structure, for the flow of processes and the orchestration of tasks and teams, comes to the fore. The symphony of a well-run organisation is music to my ears, and contributing to this harmony is a role I embrace with both hands.

Communication, the bridge between minds and hearts, is another arena where I have felt the stirrings of innate gifting. Whether this is perspective or something more innate, I've come to realise the power of words and the importance of dialogue. The gift of negotiation, an offshoot of this communicative prowess, is where I find a particular strength. The dance of negotiation, the give and take, the understanding and influencing, is a craft I have honed with each encounter.

Each of these gifts – wisdom, strategic thinking, leadership, administration, management, communication, negotiation – forms a thread in the intricate weave of who I am. They are neither singular nor isolated; they are interdependent, each one enhancing and being enhanced by the others. And like all gifts, they have grown more refined through use, through challenges faced, and through the continuous journey of learning and self-reflection.

As we dig into the exploration of our own gifts, it is crucial to acknowledge and appreciate the plurality of gifts we each possess. It is often said that variety is the spice of life, and so it is with our personal gifts. They blend to create a unique flavour, a distinct signature that is ours alone to offer to the world.

What is A Gift?

A gift is something that is given. A gift is a natural ability or talent that an individual possesses, which can be nurtured and developed to serve others and achieve personal fulfilment. Gifts are not just innate talents but also areas of potential that can be cultivated through dedication and hard work.

A gift is something that comes relatively easy to a person and distinguishes one from another. It's something that, when used effectively, allows individuals to

> *Identifying one's gift is just the beginning; the real work lies in honing that gift through continuous learning, practice, and application.*

perform at a higher level, often with a sense of joy and satisfaction. Identifying one's gift is just the beginning; the real work lies in honing that gift through continuous learning, practice, and application.

If you've ever tuned into a talent show, you'll have witnessed the raw, unpolished brilliance of undiscovered singers – individuals who step onto the stage, often with no formal training, to share their innate gifts. These are the moments that remind us of the pure, transformative power of a natural talent. There's an undeniable magic in watching someone stand before an audience, perhaps a little nervously at first, only to unleash a voice that's rich with emotion and range, capturing the hearts of all who listen.

These singers, with their gifts laid bare for all to see, exemplify the unexpected treasures that lie within us. Their stories often share a common thread: a love for music that compelled them to sing wherever they could, be it in the shower, a local choir, or the solitude of their own rooms. The stage becomes a crucible for their talent, a place where, with just the right melody, they wow the audience, the judges, and sometimes even themselves.

It's in these unscripted, genuine performances that we see the essence of a true gift. It doesn't require the validation of credentials or the polish of incessant rehearsals. Instead, it's something more innate, a spark that, when ignited by the opportunity, burns brightly enough to light up an entire auditorium.

Gifts are not learnt; they are refined. Unlike skills, which can be both acquired and honed, a gift is something you inherently possess, and your task is to refine it. You can enhance it, augment its effectiveness, and sharpen it. You can strengthen and mature it, expand its reach, and even multiply its impact. Such is the power of a gift. It is remarkably dynamic, to the extent that in the realm where you function, you may find yourself in a situation where your gift begins to reveal itself in earnest, offering you pathways and solutions in ways only a true gift can manifest.

In every chapter of my career, I've been privileged to meet individuals who carry within them a remarkable gift that seems to elevate everyone around them. At a previous organisation, I brushed shoulders with Edward - a man whose very presence seemed to charge the air with possibility. We didn't just call him a leader; we nicknamed him 'Boss', a title he wore not on a name badge, but in his aura, his approach, his every interaction.

I remember watching 'Boss' in action, this man with a natural ability to inspire and motivate. His leadership was a gift, not a skill he had consciously honed but an innate trait that flowed from him as effortlessly as breath. He didn't inspire through fear or command through authority; rather, he led by example, with empathy and an unwavering commitment to the team.

My colleagues and I were drawn to his confidence and clarity. He had this unique talent for making each of us feel valued and understood. With 'Boss' at the helm, we were not just a team; we became a collective with a shared vision, each of us integral to the journey and invested in our common goals.

This gift of leadership 'Boss' possessed was more than just the ability to manage. It was the ability to truly see people, to connect with them and to bring out the latent potential that lay dormant within. He taught me that to lead is to serve, to uplift, and to galvanise not just the mind, but the spirit of the team.

While gifts are the inherent talents we are born with, skills are often developed through experience and practise, honed over time to complement our natural gifts. It's the interplay between our innate abilities and our cultivated skills that empowers us to excel and fulfil our potential. Let's define skills.

What is a Skill?

Defining skills can be a nuanced task, as they intertwine with gifts in a complex dance. A skill is an ability or expertise developed through training and practice over time. It's a learned capacity to perform tasks with a high degree of competence, often acquired through experience or education. While some skills may indeed stem from innate gifts – abilities that we are born with and which come naturally to us – skills, unlike gifts, can be cultivated by anyone willing to put in the effort to learn and improve.

For instance, swimming is typically considered a skill because it involves learning techniques and building physical strength and endurance through practice. However, some individuals may take to the water with natural ease, suggesting a gift for swimming that precedes formal training. These natural inclinations, when refined through discipline and training, can transform an inborn gift into a developed skill.

Consider a child who can keep rhythm without ever being taught, suggesting a gift for music. As that child receives formal training and practices deliberately, the gift evolves into a skill – a mastery of music that is both innate and honed. This concept applies across various fields, from the arts to sports to communication. For example, while effective communication can be taught as a skill, there are those for whom persuasive speech is a natural gift. In both cases, whether it's a gift or an acquired skill, the end goal is to refine and enhance that ability to add value to one's endeavours and potentially, to profit from it.

Therefore, while all skills can be developed with training and practice, not all are derived from a gift. And while all gifts hold the potential to be polished into skills, they start as something given, an innate ability that provides a foundation upon which one can build.

The intention of this book is not to elevate skills above gifts or the other way around. Rather, it seeks to assist you in discerning whether your proficiencies are rooted in innate gifts or skills honed through experience – or possibly a blend of the two. It's about understanding how to deploy these qualities to your advantage as you traverse the path of life. By acknowledging and cultivating your distinct talents, you can steer your journey with increased discernment and intent, utilising your gifts and skills to attain fulfilment and make a significant contribution.

Identifying Your Gifts In *This Space*

Unearthing the treasures of your innate abilities need not be a complex quest. It starts with a simple introspection into the activities that light up your spirit and the tasks that flow from you as effortlessly as the river meets the sea. To guide you on this journey of gift-discovery, here are reflective questions to help you identify your gifts:

- **Natural Ease:** What are the tasks that you perform with such ease that they feel like second nature to you?

- **Timeless Joy:** In which activities do you find yourself so deeply immersed that time ceases to exist?

- **Intrinsic Motivation:** Are there endeavours you would joyfully undertake without the appeal of financial gain or applause?

- **Sought-After Proficiency:** Do others often seek your expertise in a particular area, recognising a proficiency that seems innate to you?

- **Distinctiveness in a Crowd:** What responsibilities do you approach with a flair that others find daunting?

- **Fulfilment in Service:** Which acts of service resonate so deeply within you that they bring a profound sense of fulfilment?

The Active Journey

The path to revealing and enhancing your gifts in *this space* is dynamic and participative. It involves exploring various roles and responsibilities, discerning where your strengths truly lie, and then advancing down that path with determination and enthusiasm. In doing so, you not only uncover your gifts but also cultivate them, thereby enriching not just your own existence but also the lives of those you touch.

As you navigate through *this space*, remember that identifying your gifts is the first step on the incredible journey of finding *your place*.

The Impact Of Your Gift In *This Space*

The value we bring to any role or function is inherently linked to the gifts we possess. It's essential that we let our gifts shine and be utilised to ensure our relevance and impact.

Firstly, the significance of our gifts lies in their ability to add value to our lives and imbue them with meaning. They are tools for self-improvement, allowing us to enhance the quality of our service and elevate our influence. Our gifts instil a sense of uniqueness and confidence, setting us apart in a crowd. When a specific skill is mentioned, it's your name that will come to mind if you've mastered that gift.

These inherent talents drive us towards fulfilment. The Bible itself speaks to this, noting that a person who is diligent in their work will stand before kings; our gifts, therefore, not only put us against the ordinary but also elevate us to places of significance.

Consider why some individuals become irreplaceable within a team. It s not merely a matter of personal preference but the undeniable gifts they contribute. Their presence adds immeasurable value, enhancing the collective strength of the organisation. Take, for example, Lionel Messi, who, instead of retiring, chose to continue his career in America. His enduring celebration is rooted in his extraordinary gift, which he continues to display with excellence, making his contribution invaluable.

It's through our gifts that we become indispensable, both to ourselves and to the world at large. They are not just personal attributes but are instrumental in shaping the broader landscape of any organisation or society in which we are involved.

> *It's through our gifts that we become indispensable, both to ourselves and to the world at large. They are not just personal attributes but are instrumental in shaping the broader landscape of any organisation or society in which we are involved.*

It's Time To Unleash Your Gift!

You do not need to hold a high position to make a meaningful contribution to society. What is essential is that you possess something the world is in search of - and it is your gift that will bring it to light.

It's time to unleash your gift! As a man or woman, you need to release your skills and gifts in every aspect of life, including business. Your unique gifts are not merely tools for personal growth and self-improvement; they are indispensable in entrepreneurship, helping to distinguish your offerings in the marketplace.

In government, too, we seek leaders who are not only well-educated and well-versed in the mechanics of governance but who also demonstrate a deep, gifted understanding of their roles. Some individuals can tackle a project with such finesse that they convince and influence with ease. This persuasive power is often rooted in one's gifts – especially in areas like awareness raising, decision-making, and conflict resolution.

Consider how certain skills intertwine deeply with our personal missions – these are the gifts that support us on our journey towards accomplishment. They foster diligence, encourage integrity, and bolster our path through life, becoming a source of significance. Think of Cristiano Ronaldo or Michael Jordan; their innate gifts have been instrumental to their legendary statuses.

Whether you're a business owner, a freelancer, or a civil servant, every system – no matter its size or complexity – requires a fusion of gifts to advance. We're all striving to complete tasks and fulfil purposes that go beyond mere profit-making. Business, at its core, is about serving others.

This is the essence of what I wish to convey: an understanding of how our gifts operate and how they can be harnessed. By recognising and nurturing your gifts, you play a crucial role in moving any endeavour forward, be it a personal goal, a community project, or a global initiative.

Chapter 3 Highlights

- A gift is an inherent ability or talent that distinguishes individuals, providing a natural capacity to perform at a higher level with a sense of joy and satisfaction.

- Unlike skills that can be acquired, a gift is something innate, refined through continuous learning, practice, and application, serving as a foundation for personal growth and contribution.

- Each gift – be it wisdom, leadership, strategic thinking, administration, management, communication, or negotiation – is interdependent, enhancing and being enhanced by others.

- Gifts are seeds that, when nurtured, grow beyond imagination, pushing through challenges and blossoming to impact the world.

Chapter 4

Your Gift And Leadership

"Leadership is not about titles, positions or flowcharts. It is about one life influencing another." **John C Maxwell**

This Space; Your Place

Leadership in *your place* is not merely about holding a position of power; it's about recognising the urgent call for change and harnessing your unique gifts to steer that transformation. Let us discuss the critical role your innate talents play in shaping effective leadership. It explores how personal gifts, when aligned with leadership roles, can become powerful catalysts for purposeful change and the achievement of collective aspirations, transcending the constraints of present situations or circumstances.

When contemplating the intersection of gift and leadership, it is essential to preface the discussion of a leader's qualities with an understanding of how one can harness their gifts to yield results, accomplish tasks, or fulfil a purpose. It is vital to acknowledge that there often exists a deep-seated yearning, a fervent desire, or an intense longing to resolve an issue – something that burns within, a gap you're eager to fill. This inner drive sets you apart, propelling you from the midst of your environment to take on a challenge, to shoulder a responsibility that calls for your attention. It is in this capacity that you emerge as a leader in the specific place where you feel this burden.

As you begin to engage with your community or society, you

strive not solely for personal gain but to effect change for the greater good, altering the prevailing narrative and challenging the status quo. True leadership involves seizing the initiative, embracing the responsibility to transform the environment.

Within this practical leadership framework, you actively create and innovate, adding value within an organisation, society, family, or even within your personal sphere. Confronted with an undesirable situation or narrative – including the stories you tell about yourself or the environment you inhabit – you have the power to enact change. Leadership, in this sense, is about reinvention and the recreation of your surroundings, spurring you into action.

Leading With Your Gift

In the heart of every great endeavour lies the pulse of leadership, the courage to embrace a calling that may seem larger than life. Such was the story of Nehemiah and the walls of Jerusalem. It took only a single individual, a man of seemingly no significant standing, who needed to request permission before he could embark on his mission. Yet, Nehemiah embraced a leadership role with such natural grace. Prior to this, he wasn't known as a governor, but through his passion and a sense of responsibility he willingly shouldered, he swiftly developed – or perhaps revealed – his innate gift for building and organising. With a clear purpose fuelling his actions, Nehemiah galvanised the people, guiding them to restore Jerusalem's walls. His story exemplifies the essence of service: utilising one's gifts to unite and lead others towards a common goal.

Leading with your gift is a profound concept that speaks to the very core of individual purpose and contribution. Your gift is not just a talent or an ability; it is your unique form of leadership, a means through which you can influence and guide others within your sphere of responsibility.

Each person is crafted with a set of skills and passions that are as unique as their fingerprints.

These intrinsic abilities are not random; they align with a particular calling or responsibility that we are meant to undertake. When we step into our area of calling, whether it's a professional field, a social cause, or a personal mission, we are stepping into our leadership role.

> *Each person is crafted with a set of skills and passions that are as unique as their fingerprints. These intrinsic abilities are not random; they align with a particular calling or responsibility that we are meant to undertake*

Leadership, in this context, is not confined to titles or positions within an organisation. It is about making an impact, about taking charge in the areas where we are most naturally gifted. Whether it's through eloquence, strategic thinking, or the capacity to inspire, your gift is the tool through which you exert influence and instigate change.

Think about the concept of leadership as service. It's a service to a cause, to a vision, or to a group of people. For instance, if your gift is the ability to articulate ideas clearly, you may find yourself as the voice for those who struggle to be heard. If you can strategise, your gift may lead you to solve complex problems in business or community planning.

Indeed, the need for leadership extends beyond public recognition. In families, in friendships, and even in mentoring relationships, leadership is exercised through the gifts we bring to these interactions. Being a leader in one aspect doesn't preclude you from being a follower in another. It's a dynamic interplay where, at times, even a mentor learns from their mentee. This exchange of roles is the essence of relational dynamics, where leadership is fluid and reciprocal.

In essence, leading with your gift is recognising that leadership is not just about authority; it's about authenticity and service. It's about using what is inherently yours – your talents, your voice, your vision – to uplift, guide, and empower. It is, in every sense, the purest expression of who you are, translated into action that benefits not just yourself, but the world around you.

To lead effectively with your gift, you must first understand your burden. What is the problem that consumes you? What keeps you up at night, stirs your emotions, leaves you feeling unsupported, empty, and drained? Identifying this is to understand your purpose. When you take responsibility to initiate change, you embrace a leadership role. Purpose is recognising the problem and committing to its solution. Let's discuss what you need to lead well with your gift:

> *When you take responsibility to initiate change, you embrace a leadership role. Purpose is recognising the problem and committing to its solution.*

Refine Your Gift: It is imperative to refine and develop your personal leadership gifts with purpose. This involves honing the innate abilities that empower you to lead effectively and make a tangible difference. It is through this process that you can truly step into your potential as a leader, equipped to inspire change and wield your unique gifts with intention. For example Tiger Woods, during his prime, it is reported that his practice and training could easily exceed 40-50 hours per week. He spent time improving his gift of golf.

Develop Capacity To Deal With Complex Situations: To thrive as a leader, one must cultivate the ability to navigate and steer through intricate and often unclear circumstances. This means mastering the art of tactical leadership in scenarios that lack transparency, where confusion reigns and clarity seems like a distant mirage. In such muddied waters, disparate voices may offer conflicting narratives, rendering the truth elusive and solutions intangible.

The hallmark of true leadership lies not merely in the identification of these challenges but in the resolute pursuit of resolution. As an emerging influencer determined to enact change, you must develop the capacity to dissect these complexities, to bring order to chaos. Your role is to be the beacon that guides through the fog of uncertainty, to make sense of the senseless, and to forge a path where others see an impasse.

In the furnace of confusion, your leadership must be the crucible that transforms uncertainty into strategy, obscurity into direction, and complexity into opportunity. It is this ability to not just endure but to lead amidst the undefined and the tumultuous that will set you apart as a leader equipped for the demands of a world that yearns for clarity and direction.

Develop Capacity To Perceive: The capacity to truly perceive is an indispensable attribute of leadership. Vision is not solely a function of the eyes; indeed, many possess sight but lack vision. They observe, yet they fail to perceive. Similarly, countless individuals have the faculty of hearing, yet they do not listen. In the cacophony of life, where many are overwhelmed by the clamour around them, it is the discerning leader who can perceive the underlying issues amidst the tumult.

Such leaders possess the rare ability to retreat into contemplation and discern possibilities where others see insurmountable problems. They can differentiate between mere noise and meaningful signals, identifying opportunities for change where others sense only despair. It is this perceptive insight that enables leaders to guide others, pointing out avenues for progress amidst the apparent impasse.

Whether in the realm of family, personal development, business, governance, or societal engagement, the skill to step back and see beyond the immediate is invaluable. The capacity to envision solutions, to transform challenges into stepping stones, is what sets a true leader apart. Perception is not a passive act; it requires an intimate understanding of the issues at hand, a clarity of thought that can cut through complexity to reveal a path forward.

This keen perception is integral to leadership, for it is by envisioning a reality beyond the present struggles that a leader can inspire change and redirect the narrative. Even in the most turbulent times, such as in the aftermath of conflict, a leader with the gift of perception can forge peace from the ashes of war. It is about seeing the latent solutions within problems, recognising the potential for reconciliation even when discord seems rife. A leader perceives, anticipates, and acts, transforming potential into reality.

Be Optimistic: Embrace optimism. As a leader, it is paramount to foster a positive outlook, no matter the circumstances. Your words should be a vessel for hope, offering reassurance that though today may be challenging, tomorrow holds new promise. The ability to lift spirits and instil a sense of expectancy for a brighter future is not just inspiring – it's transformative.

Your voice has the power to alter perceptions, to turn the tide of doubt into waves of possibility. Recognising this profound influence, a true leader wields optimism as a strategic tool, not as mere cheerfulness but as a catalyst for change. By sustaining hope, you energise and fortify those around you, empowering them to persevere.

I often remind those who are beleaguered by life's trials that adversity is transient. "This too shall pass," I assure them, "and things will undoubtedly improve." It is this conviction that we must hold onto – the conviction that we remain steadfast because hope endures. Never lower your guard, never succumb to despair. Continue to strive; each new day brings with it another opportunity to make a significant impact. Just one more effort could be the turning point, the moment that rewrites your story.

Enhance The Capacity To Function: A leader must possess the capacity to function – this is non-negotiable. It's not enough to simply assume a position of leadership; one must engage in purposeful, directed activities that resonate with intent and drive. True leadership is proven amidst continual disruptive circumstances. It is during such times that a leader's true capacity is tested. To guide individuals through tumultuous times – when they are entrenched in discomfort, yearning for change, burdened with the weight of their circumstances – is the hallmark of genuine leadership.

Consider the upheaval wrought by the worldwide pandemic of 2020: routines were overturned, the familiar became foreign, and navigating the new landscape was fraught with uncertainty. For many, this period epitomised continuous disruption, stretching over months, even years. Only leaders with the fortitude to function could steer their people, their organisations, even their governments, through such turbulence.

Leaders are tasked with guiding others through pressures, frustrations, repeated setbacks, and the crippling grip of fear. They must lend their strength to those who have been silenced, marginalised, or incapacitated. It is their duty to restore shape to what has been distorted, to realign society with its course, and to chart the path forward amidst chaos.

In the corporate realm, this resilience translates to business continuity – ensuring that operations persevere despite disorder. Governments, too, must maintain functionality amidst upheaval, whether from civil unrest, natural disasters, or other disruptive events.

On a personal level, consider the individual who has endured profound loss. Such grief can hollow out one's spirit, leaving them to navigate a life profoundly altered. Yet, the capacity to continue, to find balance – albeit precariously – is vital. The man who mourns deeply yet moves forward does so by drawing upon reserves of strength, often with the aid of support networks and therapy, to remain steadfast. Everybody has their own grief journey, but what you choose to do with it is what matters - that's how you find purpose.

What are the essential qualities one must possess or develop to lead others effectively by leveraging one's gift?

1. Ability to empower others.

Empowerment stands central to leadership. An empowered team is informed, educated, and aware – these are the seeds of growth and innovation. A leader must foster an environment that encourages critical thinking. After all, the ability to think is not just an asset; it is a necessity for navigating life's complexities.

Think of problem-solving as a skill honed by the mind's capacity to analyse and synthesise. It's a dual-edged sword, for the same cognitive processes that can extricate us from a quandary can just as easily ensnare us in one. Hence, a leader must not only possess the aptitude for empowerment but also the strategic insight to guide and extricate others from predicaments.

2. Sharing wisdom.

Sharing wisdom is another cornerstone. It's not merely about dispensing advice; it's about providing direction through knowledge. This is why people of all ages gravitate towards a leader – they recognise the value in their counsel. They find perspectives they hadn't considered, solutions to issues they couldn't resolve. The wisdom of a leader doesn't discriminate by age or experience; it serves all who seek it.

> *As a leader, your influence should extend beyond the immediate. Help others find their purpose as you have found yours. In doing so, you enable them to enrich their lives and by extension, the lives of those around them.*

As a leader, your influence should extend beyond the immediate. Help others find their purpose as you have found yours. In doing so, you enable them to enrich their lives and by extension, the lives of those around them.

Recently, I found myself confronted with an enigmatic

warning light on my car's dashboard. It was a symbol I hadn't encountered before, and it turned a routine drive into a moment of anxiety. With no knowledge of what it might signify and the manual nowhere to be found, I was momentarily at a loss.

However, I then remembered how often wisdom and guidance are at our fingertips, thanks to the shared knowledge on the internet. Pulling over, I quickly turned to YouTube on my phone, searching for insight into this unexpected dashboard mystery.

To my relief, I discovered a video by an automotive enthusiast. She had created a detailed tutorial addressing this very issue, sharing not just what the light meant but also providing step-by-step guidance on how to diagnose the problem further. Her video has amassed millions of views showing how important it is to share your wisdom.

In that moment, that youtuber's gift – her gift, passion for cars and her eagerness to educate others was invaluable. It was a potent reminder that when we share our wisdom, we empower others to navigate their challenges, turning obstacles into manageable hurdles. Her willingness to share her expertise transformed my confusion into a learning moment, allowing me to address the issue calmly and effectively.

3. Trust and transparency.

Trust and transparency are fundamental – how can one foster relationships without trust? When you are clear in your intentions and actions, you instil trust. Transparency means that others can see your methods and choose to emulate them, without concealment or deceit.

Moreover, it is crucial to appreciate and understand the diverse ways in which people perceive and learn. Individuals vary in their speed of comprehension, their backgrounds, and their foundational knowledge. Perception is a complex matter and cannot be oversimplified. One must patiently guide others towards improvement, not through manipulation, but by empowering them to make informed decisions based on the knowledge and options you have presented or made accessible to them.

4. Knowledge and confidence.

As a leader utilising your gift, you must be well-informed. This encompasses issue-specific knowledge, factual understanding, and having reliable references at your disposal. Such knowledge underpins your confidence, allowing you to speak not only from a position of understanding but also with conviction. Knowledge and confidence together empower you to drive improvement, productivity, and change, applicable at any societal level – in business, governance, family, or personal development.

The ability to motivate others towards tangible results is crucial. For example, when people seek my advice, I listen attentively, identifying gaps in their narratives that offer opportunities for change. The process of asking probing questions facilitates critical thinking, which in turn leads to innovative solutions. Motivating people towards results is not just about providing answers; it's about inspiring them to think differently and to act. If I am unable to assist directly, I consider who among my contacts might. There is always a path forward, and as a leader, it is imperative to uncover it.

Additionally, the capacity for problem-solving and decision-making is vital. Critical thinking is a necessity across all sectors, not just in business or government. Decisions can be challenging, such as relocating a family or changing job locations. Such decisions require careful thought and are indicative of a leader's ability to navigate complex situations.

Chapter 4 Highlights

- True leadership isn't a position or merely holding power; it's recognising the need for change and using your unique gifts to drive that transformation.

- A leader's effectiveness is tied to their passion and inner drive, which compels them to take responsibility for and address pressing issues within their sphere.

- Our gifts make us invaluable, not just to ourselves, but to the world.

- Effective leadership requires refining one's unique abilities and developing resilience to navigate complex and challenging situations.

Chapter 5

The Importance Of Purpose

"The greatest tragedy in life is not death, but a life without purpose." **Myles Munroe**

This Space; Your Place

As I stood at the crossroads of my life's journey, the clarity of purpose cut through everything that I have been involved in. I see now that the roles I fulfilled in the past were not mere isolated tasks; they were stepping stones, leading me towards a greater sense of purpose. My past endeavours, though different in nature, have been instrumental in shaping the path I tread today.

There came a pivotal moment when clarity dawned upon me – a realisation that transcended the confines of my previous work. It was not a question of bettering my position or seeking a larger stage for recognition, but rather a profound understanding that I was in search of a place where my unique abilities could flourish. The revelation was liberating: it mattered not how crowded the field of my endeavours became, for there is a place for everyone. Even in the most saturated spaces, there exists a spot distinctly yours, awaiting your claim.

So, I pitched my tent in the territory where my potential could be expressed, in a place where opportunity met readiness. The moment I grasped the power of my voice to guide, to enlighten, to influence decisions, was the moment I embraced my true purpose. Purpose is that driving force that compels us to seek tangible outcomes, to yearn for the testimony that our actions have indeed sparked a change. It is that unyielding desire to leave an indelible mark, to be the catalyst in transforming the ordinary into the extraordinary. Purpose is found in *your place* in *this space*.

Defining Purpose

Purpose is not just about personal ambitions or goals; it's about making a difference in the lives of others. Purpose is *your place* that is found at the intersection of passion, mission, vocation, and profession – where what you love to do, what the world needs, what you are good at, and what you can be paid for come together. Purpose is the reason why you are here.

Purpose can be succinctly described as the 'why' for our actions, the compelling why that underpins our very existence. It is the driving force behind our endeavours, be they personal or professional. Purpose imbues meaning into all that we do, from the simplest of tools to the most complex of business ventures.

Purpose is the very essence of our existence. It is the underpinning reason behind our actions, the 'why' that gives context to our lives. It answers the fundamental questions: Why are we here? What are we meant to do? Purpose defines our place in the world, such as why one is born into a particular family or resides within a certain nation.

Understanding purpose is about recognising our capabilities as well as our limitations. It is about discerning what we should do and, equally importantly, what we should not. This clarity ensures that we utilise things as they are intended, preventing misuse or abuse. For instance, medication taken outside its prescribed purpose can lead to abuse; similarly, using an electronic device contrary to its design is a misuse.

To comprehend purpose is to understand the role things play within a system or creation. Why things are the way they are, why they have been created, why systems function as they do – this is the essence of purpose. And this concept of purpose is intertwined with the notion of a Creator, the origin from which life springs forth. Therefore, as we grow and gain consciousness, it becomes our responsibility to uncover and discover our unique purpose in life.

Consider your motivations behind anything. During a recent business consultation, I engaged with a client eager to embark on a new entrepreneurial journey. Curious about the impetus for this venture, I posed the question: "Why do you wish to start this business?" His response was straightforward yet revealing: "I'm looking to make some extra money."

This answer, while honest, shed light on a common misconception. For many, a business is seen merely as a vehicle for income, a means to an end. However, this perspective often overlooks the essence of entrepreneurship, which is to create value through solving problems or fulfilling needs.

I explained to my client that a business should be driven by more than just the pursuit of financial gain. It should stem from a purpose, a desire to serve and to contribute. When a business is founded on the principle of service, it naturally attracts customers. Financial success, in such cases, becomes a by-product of the value provided.

Businesses driven by a mere desire for profit tend to falter when financial rewards diminish. In essence, purpose gives you direction. It is the undercurrent that propels us forward, instilling our actions with significance and direction.

Purpose Will Give You A Place

Purpose will give you a place even in a very tight and narrow space. In a world awash with roles and identities, your purpose carves out a distinct place for you – a position where passion meets action, where your calling becomes your hallmark. This place transcends mere geographical location; it resonates with your environment, aligns with your profession, and echoes the discipline you embody. It's inextricably linked to your deepest interests, the things you are drawn to not by chance, but by design.

Consider the spaces you occupy – your nation, your community, your family, your vocation. These aren't just coordinates on a map; they are the arenas where you express your purpose. Your passion marks the territory where you are meant to thrive, regardless of the crowd that surrounds you. For it is not about the occupation of space, but the assertion of place.

You may look around and see an industry brimming with talent, a niche seemingly overflowing with voices. Yet, do not be daunted. In the noise of the crowd, it's your unique purpose that will cut through the noise. It's not about displacing others; it's about discovering your rightful place amidst them. Even in the most saturated of environments, there is room for you!

Your purpose is the force that distinguishes you, that defines the essence of your gift. It doesn't matter how constricted the space appears; *your place* within it is assured, waiting for you to claim it.

The Importance Of Purpose

In the pursuit of purpose, patience becomes your ally. Challenges and setbacks are universal, yet they are not the end. Purpose infuses resilience, it fuels determination, and it breathes life into the seemingly insurmountable. It's the internal compass that guides you to stand firm, to reinvent, and to emerge triumphant.

Your purpose will secure you a place, even within the narrowest of margins. It beckons you to explore, to take root, and to flourish in the very essence of who you are meant to be. Purpose is the promise that in a crowded space, you will always find *your place*.

I was out shopping with my family and I noticed something interesting as I walked past the oral health aisle of the supermarket. I was intrigued by the array of toothpaste varieties on display. From whitening formulas to enamel repair, each tube claims its own unique place on the shelf. And just when you think there couldn't possibly be room for more, a new brand emerges, boasting yet another innovative feature.

This abundance is a compelling reminder that there is room for your idea, your gift, in this vast space. Just like each toothpaste finds its niche catering to specific dental needs, your unique contribution has its own audience waiting. The market's capacity to welcome new entrants is a clear signal that your distinctive offering has the potential to carve out its rightful spot.

How Purpose Contributes To A Fulfilled Life

A life well spent is a life where purpose is fulfilled. Life devoid of purpose is akin to a ship adrift at sea. Existence, stripped of meaning, becomes an idle state, much like objects gathered dust in an unvisited corner of a house. We acquire things because they serve a purpose, fulfil a need. Consider the car purchase: one chooses a reliable vehicle capable of long motorway journeys not merely as a possession but as a vital tool for life's ventures.

Purpose breathes life into our days. It propels us beyond mere existence towards a vibrant life of deliberate action. When you anchor every deed to a purpose, you set forth on a voyage to achieve what you were placed here to accomplish. Life, then, is not just about being; it's about becoming – fulfilling the very essence of your being.

A life suffused with purpose is not content with simple existence; it seeks to manifest the very reasons for its being. With a clear purpose, your talents and passions become the engines of

The Importance Of Purpose

your journey, guiding you to a destination replete with satisfaction and fulfilment. Because when you are on a mission, life transcends routine – it becomes a service.

Life, in its very essence, is designed to be purposeful. It's not the struggles of existence that define us, but rather the steadfast pursuit of our calling. Purpose is not a hindrance to enjoyment; on the contrary, it enriches every experience by infusing it with significance.

Those who live with purpose are the ones who, even in the face of life's impermanence, strive to complete their mission. They are not driven by a fear of death but motivated by the legacy they aspire to leave. Such individuals set their lives in order, ensuring their impact resonates beyond their presence.

The journey towards purpose begins with a decision, one that should be rooted in well-informed choices and a clear understanding of the situation at hand. It is essential to arm yourself with knowledge before embarking on this path. When you are well-informed, your decisions carry weight; they are made with conviction and without the shadow of regret.

This is a message I often convey in my conversations: I am not discouraging you from pursuing your aspirations, but I urge you not to base your actions on assumptions or speculations. Avoid hasty judgments and the allure of seemingly promising shortcuts. Instead, strive for a thorough understanding and a solid foundation. Approach your purpose with the due diligence it deserves, ensuring that each step you take is deliberate and informed.

Relocating from Nigeria to the UK marked a significant turning point in my life. Admittedly, the move was tough, but not in the way you might expect. The challenge lay not within me, but in the eyes of my peers, particularly from an economic standpoint. They questioned the seriousness of my decision, but for me, it was one of the clearest choices I've ever made.

The true struggle wasn't in the decision itself but in the process of transitioning from one life to another, from the familiar to the unknown. Yet, this phase was less of a struggle and more of a natural progression for me. It was a seamless step driven by a deep-seated zeal and an awareness of the potential that awaited.

I've not once looked back with regret or second-guessed my choice. Starting afresh in a new place was daunting, yet it was a challenge I accepted with open arms, fuelled by an inner fire and the drive to succeed. I was confident that it wouldn't be long before I found my footing. My past experiences, the circle of life I cherish, and the gifts I possess, combined with the opportunities around me, assured me that I was on the right path. Stepping onto new soil, I was ready to plant my feet firmly and begin anew.

A life infused with purpose is not just one that exists – it truly lives. It's a life where every action is a step towards fulfilment, where every day is a canvas for meaningful expression. To live with purpose is to carve a path that leads not only to personal happiness but also to the enrichment of others.

Chapter 5 Highlights

- Every past role has been a stepping stone to a greater purpose and a place where their unique abilities can shine.

- Purpose is the intersection of passion, mission, vocation, and profession, acting as the driving force that infuses actions with meaning and direction.

- There is a distinct place for everyone's purpose, ensuring that each person can find their niche and make a unique contribution, regardless of any apparent saturation within your chosen sphere.

- Living with purpose transforms existence from mere survival to a journey of impactful actions and fulfilling one's reason for being.

Chapter 6

Discovering Your Place

"Purpose is the most important motivator in the world. The reason for doing something rates much higher than the reward or the punishment. Your purpose is doing what you love to do."

Bob Proctor

This Space; Your Place

Discovering and stepping into one's place of purpose is a journey that many find daunting, especially when weighed down by the opinions of others. The truth is, if you haven't walked in those shoes, faced those hurdles, and borne the weight of societal expectations, it's challenging to comprehend the courage it takes to pursue what truly makes you happy.

Everyone seeks happiness, yet many become ensnared in pursuits that only mimic the form of joy. They hop from one endeavour to the next, leaving a trail of unfinished tasks, not because they lack the ability, but because they haven't found what they're truly searching for. This ceaseless quest can often be misinterpreted as indecision or a lack of drive, but more commonly, it's a lack of patience and self-awareness.

If your purpose is clear, resilience becomes second nature. It's not the absence of fear or doubt, but the conviction that the path you've chosen is worth the perseverance. The pivotal question, then, is not 'What do others want for me?' but 'What do I want for myself?'

This question, simple yet profound, can be a beacon through the fog of uncertainty. It isn't about the immediacy of money or the convenience of any job at hand. It's about aligning with your inner compass, even if that means temporarily fulfilling obligations to pave the way for your true calling.

I recall a time when I was in roles that didn't resonate with my ultimate goals. I, too, had to pay the bills. Yet, in those very roles, I found clarity. In meetings fraught with tension, I could smile, knowing that our shared location was not indicative of our shared direction. We each had our distinct destinations, much like passengers on a train. The train stops, people alight, but the train continues its journey regardless.

When you find yourself in a space shared with others, remember: respect and politeness go a long way. You're all on a journey, but not necessarily to the same place. And that's alright.

Recently, I witnessed the power of purpose in action. Clients of mine, who had started their business from the humble beginnings of their home, had transformed their passion into a thriving enterprise. Their dedication was evident in every pastry they baked, every van they sent out. When I suggested they could expand further, they were elated. Their success wasn't just about the financial gain; it was about the fulfilment of doing what they loved, serving their community, and heeding my advice to better their enterprise.

This is the essence of purpose – not just doing what is expected, but what ignites your passion. It's about sitting back and asking yourself, "What do I truly want? Where do I see myself?" It's not about the qualifications you lack or the expectations of others. It's about starting where you are, with what you have, and nurturing that seed of desire.

So, cast aside the doubts, the 'shoulds', and the whispers of inadequacy. Your purpose doesn't shout over the noise; it's a steady, guiding voice that says, "This is the way, walk in it." Start small, dream big, and step by step, you'll find yourself not just where you want to be, but where you're meant to be, living life to the fullest. That, after all, is what purpose does – it carves out a space for you in the tapestry of life, a space that's uniquely yours. It doesn't necessarily matter where or how you started, but what matters is where and how you finish.

Steps To Discovering Your Purpose

The Bible gives an insightful proverb which says, that the purposes of a person's heart are deep waters, but one who has insight draws them out. What you really want in life is hidden like treasure underwater. To find it, you need to dive deep and look closely. The verse tells us that understanding our true purpose isn't always easy; it's hidden deep inside us like the bottom of the ocean.

But if we are wise and take the time to understand ourselves, we can bring our true purpose to the surface. Just like a diver who finds pearls in the sea, we can discover the special reason we're here – our own unique purpose. It takes patience and courage to search for it, but when we do, we can make our lives and the lives of others better.

The first question that one needs to ask as they seek to discover their place in life is, **"Why am I here?"** This is not a dialogue to be broadcast, but rather a private conference with oneself, without the distractions of others' paths, opinions and achievements. It's an introspection that requires honesty, free from the noise of comparison.

> *The first question that one needs to ask as they seek to discover their place in life is,* ***"Why am I here?"***

From childhood, where dreams are as pliable as clay, we articulate our desires. Even in my earliest memories, I find myself sensitive to the words I spoke. In those days of youthful education, my assertions of who I wished to become were more than idle chatter; they were propellants, steering me subtly yet surely.

As we grow, these early desires evolve, honed by our experiences and the essence of who we are. Society too casts its influence, presenting countless labels and roles, each subject to cultural tides. Nevertheless, the essence of our true intent often endures beyond such external definitions.

Acknowledging and pursuing our purpose is pivotal to a life lived fully. It is a vital quest for clarity, a need to decipher the 'why' that underscores our existence. This is a mission we must undertake with sincerity and dedication.

We are tasked to sift through the noise, to find that resonant note that aligns with our individual essence. This is not an idle quest; it is as crucial as the heartbeat, a central pillar of a meaningful existence. To discover why we are here is a serious and profound undertaking, one that defines the very quality of our lives.

To live meaningfully, one must embrace this mission to discover purpose with open arms. It's a journey of self-discovery, a vital endeavour that shapes our identity and charts the course of our lives. It's about peering inward and answering the call that has echoed within us from the beginning, guiding us towards our life's true existence.

What Do You Really Want In Life?

In the discovery of purpose, a pivotal question arises: "What do you truly desire?" It's not merely about change or improvement; it's about unearthing those profound yearnings that resonate within you. Identifying these innermost desires is the essence of discovering what you want from life.

You see, an inward reflection is more revealing than a list of superficial wants. I'm reminded of an anecdote from my early career. Let me share with you a memory from the time when I began lecturing at the university in 1995. I was under the wing of my department head, a woman of considerable respect who served as my mentor. She dispatched me on an errand to convey a message to a professor who was the Dean of faculty, a journey that took me through the sprawling corridors of academia.

Upon completing the task and as I reached for the door to depart, the professor's voice stopped me. "Young man," she called out, her question slicing through the silence, "Do you truly wish to pursue this career?" I was taken aback. This was a woman who had no prior interactions with me, not present at my interview, outside of my faculty and department's sphere. Yet, her inquiry struck a chord.

While I affirmed my commitment, not wishing to betray any uncertainty in my fledgeling professional steps, her question lingered. Despite my dedication to the role and the valuable experience I was accruing, the truth was, I yearned for something more – different environs, yet the same pursuit of knowledge.

This is the crux of purpose discovery. It is not about aligning with others' perceptions or mirroring their pathways. It's about the personal truths that propel us. For fourteen years, I stayed in that academic role, yet eventually, my journey led me elsewhere. Though no longer lecturing, I remain an educator at heart, transforming lives through training, workshops, and influence – this is my calling.

> *This is the crux of purpose discovery. It is not about aligning with others' perceptions or mirroring their pathways. It's about the personal truths that propel us*

Had I possessed the insights I hold now, my teaching methods would have been vastly different. Education is not just about passing knowledge; it's about ensuring learning, imparting understanding, inspiring minds, and fostering real change.

Therefore, when delving into the depths of your desires, cast aside the constraints of conformity. It matters not if your dreams seem at odds with your surroundings; what matters is their authenticity to you. Once you've grasped your true desires, the journey ahead becomes one of navigation towards fulfilment, carving out a path to where you aspire to be.

Identify Your Burden

I know a respected doctor who trained and qualified in medicine and practiced for a few years. He recently left the profession to study law, as law was his true burden. A burden is something you can't shake off. In the context of purpose, the word 'burden' refers to a deep-seated concern or a compelling drive to address a particular issue or challenge that is of personal significance. It's not a burden in the sense of a cumbersome weight, but rather a powerful motivation that you feel deeply about, something that you're passionate to resolve or contribute to.

To identify your burden, there must be a problem you're compelled to solve. What is that problem? That's your burden. When we talk about solving problems, it doesn't have to be something grand like needing to be a doctor or a teacher to solve complex equations. It's about your value to your community, to yourself, and to those around you. What are you doing to elevate people's situation and bring them to a level where they will be forever grateful?

Ask yourself: What is it you can't bear to see? If you can't stand the sight of children begging for food, maybe that discomfort is guiding you towards helping orphanages. Perhaps there's something else you need to analyse to find your burden and then apportion your task accordingly.

When discovering your purpose, you might identify a problem and feel that because you're not in a position to make an immediate impact, your efforts are in vain. But that's not the case. It doesn't matter if you are in a completely different profession at the moment.

To identify your burden, find out what irritates or infuriates you the most, what makes you burn inside. This is a signal or a pointer to the problem you are meant to solve. What would you naturally do without any reward or monetary incentive? What drives you without the promise of payment? This is a key indicator of your passion. I can assure you that if someone calls you to address a problem that genuinely sparks your interest, the absence of financial reward won't deter you. Your greatness lies in how you handle or manage your inner desire.

How Do I Get There?

Embarking on the path to purpose, we invariably confront the question: **"How do I reach my destination?"** It matters not if your aspirations seem misaligned with your current circumstances. That is of no consequence. It's the pursuit that counts, and more pertinently, the journey towards attainment.

We must delve into a personal methodology, discuss the requisite protocols, and assess the needs essential for progress. What are the key elements that you must unravel to uncover your stance, to challenge the precepts you've assured yourself of? Test your theories against your fervour, gauge them with your energy, affirm them with your intrinsic sentiment. Does it resonate with your core? Scrutinise your current position against your aspirations.

Your goals should always be bigger than what you can currently achieve. They should make you aim higher. If your dream isn't much bigger than what you're already doing, it's not challenging enough. It should

> *Your goals should always be bigger than what you can currently achieve. They should make you aim higher. If your dream isn't much bigger than what you're already doing, it's not challenging enough.*

make you stop and think hard about how to make it happen. You're really starting to work towards your goals when you start asking yourself, "How can I reach this big dream?"

I am in the leadership and personal development space like many notable people. This has not stopped me from finding my place. When I listen to luminaries like John Rohn, Dale Carnegie, Tony Robbins, John Maxwell, Myles Munroe, Brian Tracy, Bob Proctor etc. I'm reminded that even they acknowledge the impossibility of reaching everyone simultaneously. Despite their expansive influence, there remain individuals yet untouched by their teachings. This realisation beckons a question of personal relevance and a journey tailored to one's unique calling. **There is a place for your voice in *this space*!** When I asked myself the question, "How do I get there?" one of the steps I took was writing this book. Another step was launching The SkillsMindset Podcast, which is available on all major podcast platforms. All of this is part of my journey as I express my purpose in *this space*.

So, if you abandon *your place* in *this space*, some people are going to die without your contribution, without purpose, without fulfilling it. You owe the world your gift.

Chapter 6 Highlights

- Discovering one's purpose requires courage, especially when facing societal pressures and expectations; it's a journey that demands self-awareness and resilience.

- People often mistake constant activity for progress, but without finding true purpose, activities can lead to a cycle of unfulfillment.

- Clarity of purpose instils resilience and shifts focus from others' expectations to one's own aspirations and happiness.

- True purpose is found not through external validation or immediate gains but through aligning with one's inner compass, even through temporary roles.

Chapter 7

Making Your Place Matter

"Your true beliefs and visions shape your reality; dare to dream boldly and passionately, for in those dreams lie the seeds of your future success."

Brian Tracy

Why did you wake up today? What is driving you through the day and the week? We all have a unique place in this world, and we must recognise and embrace it. Each one of us has the power to make a meaningful impact, not only in our own lives but also in the lives of others. Your purpose should get you up every morning.

For over a decade, I've harboured many dreams and one of them was to be a high-impact person. It's a dream that has played on the periphery of my consciousness, whispering promises of adventure, creativity, and fulfilment. As I stand on the threshold of this new chapter, I realise that my dream isn't just a fleeting desire; it's a compass guiding me towards my true purpose.

Imagine me having a dream without a plan. It soon becomes a wishful thought that fades into oblivion like a mirage that fakes the image of reality. That is why dreams indeed have a place in *this space*. Your reality starts when vision, dreams and purpose become a panoply that alters the path you travel and sets you on a pathway to a destination that not only impacts you as a person but also affects people around your defined space. Vision, dreams and purpose are three interconnected yet distinct terms that can help you define your goals and aspirations in life.

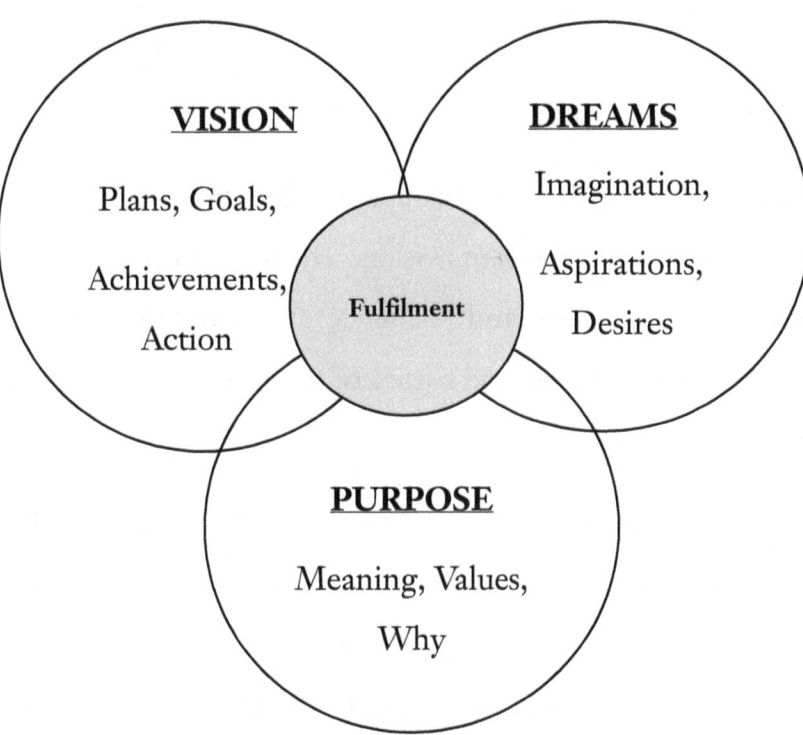

The Interconnected Path of Dream, Vision and Purpose.

The diagram above illustrates this concept. The interconnectedness of vision, dreams, and purpose. Where these meet (at the core) forms the foundation of personal fulfilment and impact. Vision shapes dreams, dreams inform purpose, and purpose gives direction to vision, creating a cohesive and aligned path towards meaningful achievements.

A fitting metaphor for this concept is a three-stranded rope where each strand represents vision, dreams, and purpose woven together. The strength and resilience of the rope symbolise the cohesive and interconnected nature of the three concepts working in harmony in your life.

Just as the strands of a rope intertwine to create a sturdy and reliable structure, so too do our vision, dreams, and purpose intertwine to provide strength and resilience in our journey through life. Each strand contributes its unique qualities to the whole, reinforcing one another and ensuring stability even in the face of challenges.

The vision strand provides direction and clarity, guiding our actions and aspirations towards a defined goal. The dreams strand

> *When you can envision what you were born to do, that becomes the guiding vision for your life.*

fuels our imagination and ambition, inspiring us to reach beyond the ordinary and strive for greatness. The purpose strand anchors us to our values and beliefs, giving meaning and significance to our endeavours.

Together, these three strands form a strong and unbreakable bond, supporting us as we navigate the twists and turns of life's journey. Just as a well-crafted rope can withstand the forces of nature, so too can our interconnected vision, dreams, and purpose empower us to overcome obstacles and achieve our fullest potential. This is how you can make your place matter. One element in isolation will not allow your potential to be maximised.

The aim of this chapter isn't to assert that vision is superior to dreams or purpose. Rather, it underscores the necessity of all three elements in achieving one's purpose. As Myles Munroe aptly put it, "Vision is purpose in pictures." When you can envision what you were born to do, that becomes the guiding vision for your life.

There's no hierarchy here; it's not about saying one is superior to another. Instead, it's about recognising that while you may harbour dreams, your vision should be clear and compelling enough to guide you towards your desired destination. Take for instance, young individuals who envision themselves achieving great feats, like aspiring to be a footballer in a particular team. With determination and effort, some find themselves playing alongside their idols within a short span of time.

Dreams are essential, but mere fantasising won't suffice. Your vision necessitates concrete action. Merely dreaming without taking steps towards actualisation renders those dreams stagnant. You may envisage distant lands and experiences, but the distinction between merely dreaming and achieving lies in action. Transforming from being a mere dreamer to an achiever requires intentionality and planning. Without strategic planning, dreams remain unfulfilled, and visions remain distant aspirations.

The journey from dreaming to realising your vision is not merely about traversing physical distance; it's about understanding your purpose. Purpose illuminates the why behind your actions, providing clarity amidst the journey towards your vision.

Doing The Things That Matter

It is John Maxwell who said, "Success is not about getting ahead, but about getting along and making a difference with what you have."

Often, people fail to recognise what they have in their hands to make the place they are in matter. To make your place matter, you need to do something that will matter – something meaningful. Here is the question: What do you have at your disposal? And the next question: What are you doing with it?

The story of Biblical Moses is a brilliant example of this. Moses was holding in his hand the thing that mattered. When he had reached the end of his wits, the Almighty asked him what he had in his hand. It was a shepherd's rod – but that same rod is what made the difference in his life and many others. Always ask yourself if what you are doing at any time and place matters; this will help you maximise your potential in any place. Make what you have matter.

Let's Explain These Terms

Vision refers to your aspirations and what you aim to achieve or create in the future. It is a clear picture and inspiring representation of your desired outcome or destination. For example, your vision may include seeing yourself as a successful entrepreneur, a worthy ambassador, exploring the world, being a champion, or making a positive impact on society. It is important to note that vision is about what you truly see, rather than what you merely want to see or be.

On the other hand, dreams encompass the things you imagine or fantasise about doing or possessing. They are more general and abstract ideas that you contemplate without taking direct action. For instance, your dreams might involve living in an ideal world, winning the lottery, meeting your favourite celebrity, or venturing into space. Dreams are about what you want to see or be, such as being a successful business owner.

Purpose, meanwhile, encapsulates the underlying reason or meaning behind your actions and choices. It serves as the driving force that motivates and guides you in pursuit of your vision and goals. Your purpose could entail helping others, expressing yourself creatively, or realising your full potential.

The relationship between Vision, Dream, and Purpose can be summarised as follows:

- Your vision is based on your dream, but it is more specific and grounded in reality. It represents what you need to actualise your dream. Moreover, your vision should align with your purpose, the underlying reason for wanting to achieve your dream.

- Your dream is derived from your purpose, but it is less defined and more idealistic. It encompasses what you aspire to accomplish or experience in life. Additionally, your dream should inspire your vision or the strategies you devise to achieve your purpose.

- Your purpose serves as the foundation for your dream and vision, providing them with direction and significance. Ultimately, your purpose should guide your dream and vision, determining what you strive for in life.

Empowering Dreams

Dreams can be seen as a foundation upon which we build our aspirations. They may initially appear as wishful thinking, where we imagine things we desire or aim to achieve. These may include ideal situations we envision ourselves in, or qualities we wish to possess. However, without action or determination, dreams may remain as mere fantasies, easily dismissed as wishful thinking or daydreaming.

For example, imagine someone dreaming of becoming a successful online content creator. At first, this dream may seem like a distant imagination, a wishful aspiration without a clear plan of action. However, if the individual takes their dream seriously and digs deeper into their aspirations, they may begin to formulate concrete goals and plans to turn their dream into reality. This involves moving beyond passive dreaming to actively pursuing their vision, aligning their actions with their purpose and dedicating themselves to the pursuit of their goals.

In essence, while dreams may start as mere thoughts or wishes, they have the potential to become effective motivators if we are willing to invest the effort and determination required to transform them into tangible achievements.

Dreams have enormous power to change the world. Did you know that Google was started from a mere dream? Larry Page had a dream of creating a powerful search engine which was inspired by his curiosity and fascination with the vast amount of information available on the internet. As a graduate student at Stanford University in the late 1990s, Page was struck by the challenge of navigating and organising this vast sea of data effectively.

During his research, Page observed that existing search engines at the time were limited in their ability to provide accurate and relevant search results. He became determined to develop a more efficient and intuitive search engine that could better serve users' needs.

Page's dream was further fuelled by his collaboration with Sergey Brin, another graduate student at Stanford. Together, they shared a passion for exploring the possibilities of organising information on the Internet in a more efficient and user-friendly manner. This was the manifestation and birth of the dream which was envisioned - it's that vision which we now know as Google.

> *Our creativity is ignited when we encounter challenges and obstacles that we must overcome.*

I want to encourage you as you navigate your path in this space not to dismiss your dreams. I strongly encourage you to always document them. Our creativity is ignited when we encounter challenges and obstacles that we must overcome. They reflect your deepest yearnings, untapped potentials, and true callings. They can uncover hidden truths, ignite your creativity, and shape your decisions. By paying attention to your dreams, interpreting them wisely, and taking action accordingly, you have the potential to transform your hopes into reality.

Keeping a dream journal demonstrates your appreciation for your dreams. I've cultivated a habit of maintaining a dream diary, using the notes app on my device to record and preserve my dreams. Some individuals have found success using dream boards.

To create a dream board, individuals gather pictures, quotes, and other visual representations that resonate with their goals and desires. These can include images of places they want to visit, people they admire, achievements they aspire to, or qualities they wish to embody. The goal is to create a visual representation of one's dreams and desires that can serve as a source of inspiration and motivation.

Once created, the dream board is often displayed in a prominent place where it can be easily seen, such as on a wall or bulletin board. By regularly viewing the dream board, individuals can reinforce their goals, stay focused on their aspirations, and maintain a positive mindset as they work towards manifesting their dreams into reality. Dream big, dream frequently, and never stop dreaming. Remember to share your dreams and stories with others, for you never know who you might inspire or what you might achieve.

Manifesting Change Through Your Dreams

Depending on what your dream is, you can envision a new version of yourself. You can dream of a new family dynamic, envision a transformed community or neighbourhood, or aim towards a better nation or society. Wherever your vision lies, begin taking steps towards it.

Some individuals have dreamed of transforming a whole country's culture. When you possess a vision or dream, and a sense of purpose, you may find yourself diverging from the norm, becoming a nonconformist. This deviation from societal norms can sometimes lead to challenges, even imprisonment. However, standing firm in your beliefs, even amidst adversity, tests the strength of your vision.

Challenges validate the authenticity of your beliefs and actions. Conversely, conformity suggests complacency and a lack of differentiation from the masses. Nonconformity may not always win you popularity, even within your own family, but it fosters a profound sense of purpose and passion. Your dream infuses you with a sense of purpose, even amidst hardship. You understand why you endure challenges and discomfort – it's for the sake of achieving your dream. This understanding is the essence of purpose. Challenges may tempt you to abandon your path, but remember, the journey towards your dream demands endurance.

Not everyone possesses the ability to dream deeply or to

envision a brighter future. Yet, without vision, there is no purpose. Without purpose, one perishes, stagnating amidst the currents of life. Embrace your vision, pursue your dreams, and let them guide you towards a purposeful existence.

I am greatly inspired by the life and story of Martin Luther King Jr. who dreamed of a society where all people would be judged by the content of their character rather than the colour of their skin. His vision for racial equality and social justice inspired millions and fuelled the civil rights movement in the United States.

Martin Luther King Jr. faced numerous challenges and hardships in his pursuit of his dream. He encountered opposition from those who sought to maintain the status quo of racial segregation and discrimination. He endured personal threats, imprisonment, and violence directed at him and his supporters.

However, King remained firm in the pursuit of justice. He understood that enduring these challenges was necessary for the sake of achieving his dream of equality.

King's big dream ultimately led to significant progress in the fight for civil rights. His leadership and perseverance inspired countless individuals to join the struggle for equality, leading to landmark legislation such as the Civil Rights Act of 1964 and the Voting Rights Act of 1965.

Self Reflections

1. What is one dream you hold dear?

   _____

   _____

   _____

   _____

2. In what ways have you experienced challenges or opposition in pursuing your own dreams, and how have these obstacles shaped your determination and resilience?

   _____

   _____

   _____

   _____

3. Imagine yourself achieving your most cherished dream. What impact do you envision it having on your life, your community, and the world at large?

_____

_____

_____

_____

The Power Of Vision

Vision is when you can see what others can't see. It goes deeper into the realm of possibility than dreams. When you possess vision, it goes beyond mere wishful thinking; it stems from a profound understanding and insight. It's as if you've glimpsed into the future, visualising yourself in a particular place or circumstance. You've witnessed the potential for change, whether it be in your surroundings or within yourself. You've seen glimpses of what is possible, and this awareness propels you forward with determination and purpose.

The power of possibility inherent in vision renders it remarkably vivid and tangible. When we envision, we conjure forth mental images that feel undeniably real to us. These images, born from the depths of our imagination, carry a profound sense of conviction. We believe in them with certainty, for they paint a picture of what could be, instilling us with the faith that our aspirations are within reach.

Vision transcends the limitations of our physical sight; it is not merely a function of our eyes but rather a manifestation of our innermost being. With vision, we perceive not with our eyes, but with our hearts and insight. Even with closed eyes, we can still 'see' the future unfold before us, guided by the inner vision that illuminates our path.

> *Where there is no vision, there is no purpose.*

This insight ignites a fire within us, propelling us to action with boundless enthusiasm and determination. With each leap of faith, we reach out to grasp the future that we have envisioned, our spirits soaring as we pursue our dreams.

Indeed, the power of vision lies not only in the images we see but in the belief they inspire and the actions they compel. It is a force that drives us forward, guiding us towards the realisation of our deepest desires and aspirations.

This Space; Your Place

Vision alters perspectives, leading to a profound realisation. As your perspective shifts, you may find yourself reconsidering your beliefs and choices. The mental images from your vision become ingrained in your mind, compelling you to bring them closer to reality. Consequently, your mindset evolves, your perception transforms, and your beliefs adapt as you are drawn towards the future depicted in your vision.

You are inspired to take action as if you have already visited your envisioned destination. You begin preparing yourself for the journey ahead, envisioning yourself in the place you aspire to reach. Similarly, when convinced of the validity of your vision, it empowers you to plan and embark on the journey towards your desired destination. Even if you've never physically experienced or seen the reality depicted in your vision, your belief in its existence propels you forward, driving you to take steps towards its realisation.

As you progress on your journey, others may notice changes in you. Your commitment to fulfilling your vision becomes evident, transforming your life in remarkable ways. Ultimately, it is purpose that fuels your determination to manifest your vision, guiding you towards a life aligned with your deepest aspirations.

Where there is no vision, there is no purpose. A life without purpose is wasted and empty. Vision gives your journey direction and uniqueness. It tells you what to do and where to go in life, while purpose defines why.

You need to know where you are heading now. Take a detour if necessary and start navigating towards your destination. Not everything and everywhere is good for you. Focus on the one or few things that truly matter and start working on them. This way, when your vision and purpose face challenges and difficult situations, you will know where you stand and why. If your vision is clear and convincing enough, you will stand by it and be known for it. People are remembered for what they stood for, not what they fell for. Let's have a look at the life of Mahatma Gandhi. His life provides numerous examples of standing by his vision despite facing challenges. One notable example is Gandhi's commitment to nonviolent resistance, also known as Satyagraha, during India's struggle for independence from British rule.

Despite facing opposition, prison, and even violence, Gandhi remained steadfast in his belief in nonviolent protest as a means to achieve political and social change. He emphasised the importance of truth and moral principles in the pursuit of justice, and he encouraged others to stand by these principles even in the face of difficulty.

Gandhi's firm commitment to his vision of nonviolence not only inspired millions of people in India but also garnered international attention and respect. He became known as a symbol of peaceful resistance and a champion of human rights, leaving a lasting legacy that continues to influence movements for social justice around the world.

We know him because he was a great visionary - he stood for his vision. Your vision takes you on a unique journey of life experiences that only you can understand and testify to. Vision gives life a purpose.

Self Reflections

1. What is your personal vision for your life, and how does it inspire and motivate you to take action?

_____

_____

_____

_____

2. How can you cultivate and nurture your inner vision to guide you towards a more purposeful and fulfilling life?

_____

_____

_____

_____

3. In what ways can you integrate the power of vision into your daily life to bring clarity, direction, and purpose to your actions and decisions?

_____

_____

_____

_____

Unveiling Purpose

Purpose is the why behind our actions, defining why we do what we do. It provides clarity on our destination, the place we aspire to reach even when it seems distant. So why the change? Why the shift in perspective and behaviour? Purpose has taken precedence. We now understand why our actions differ or why we no longer engage in certain activities. Every action, or inaction, is driven by purpose.

Why is purpose so crucial? Because it anchors us to our why – the reason behind our journey. Not every opportunity aligns with our purpose, and not every possession is necessary for the journey. A person with purpose possesses a singular focus, a steadfast commitment to reaching their destination. Amidst a sea of distractions, they remain disciplined, resolute in their pursuit. Without this discipline, they risk losing sight of their vision and failing to realise their dreams.

Fulfilment, accomplishment, and realisation stem from understanding the power of purpose. By harnessing this power, we transform our lives, creating a better future for ourselves and those around us. However, this journey is not without its challenges. It requires strong leadership, guiding us through the process, whether short or long.

In essence, purpose is the driving force behind our journey towards fulfilment. It shapes our decisions, moves us forward, and ultimately leads us to a place of contentment and joy.

A purposeful leader whose life truly mattered is Nelson

Mandela. His purpose was rooted in his commitment to ending apartheid and achieving racial equality in South Africa. Despite facing decades of incarceration, Mandela remained focussed in his dedication to this cause. His purpose served as the driving force behind his actions and decisions, providing clarity and direction even during the darkest times.

During his 27 years behind bars, Mandela demonstrated remarkable self-leadership. He maintained his integrity, dignity, and focus on his purpose, refusing to compromise his principles or abandon his vision of a free and democratic South Africa. Mandela's self-discipline and resilience inspired others both within and outside of South Africa to continue the fight against apartheid.

Upon his release from prison in 1990, Mandela emerged as a global symbol of peace, reconciliation, and leadership. He led negotiations to dismantle apartheid and transition South Africa to democracy, ultimately becoming the country's first black president in 1994.

> *Self-leadership is about self-discipline and taking proactive steps towards your goals, regardless of any challenges that may arise.*

Throughout his presidency and beyond, Mandela remained

committed to his purpose of building a united and inclusive nation. He promoted reconciliation and forgiveness, prioritising the interests of the nation over personal grievances or vendettas. Mandela's leadership, rooted in his purpose, played a pivotal role in guiding South Africa through a period of profound change and transformation.

In the journey towards fulfilment, leadership plays a pivotal role. However, it's important to recognise that leadership begins from within. You have the ability to lead yourself, to chart your own course and stay true to your purpose. Self-leadership is about self-discipline and taking proactive steps towards your goals, regardless of any challenges that may arise.

Self-leadership is not just about leading yourself; it's about staying aligned with your vision and purpose, even in the face of adversity. It's about staying focused and disciplined, ensuring that you remain on track towards your destination. This principle applies not only to individuals but also to communities, families, governments, and societies as a whole.

In self-leadership, you take ownership of your journey, empowering yourself to overcome obstacles and achieve your aspirations. It's about staying true to your vision and purpose, no matter what challenges may come your way. As you lead yourself with determination and resilience, you inspire others to do the same, creating a ripple effect of positive change in the world around you.

This concept intertwines closely with the notion of faith. While faith is often associated with religious contexts, it can be understood more broadly as the substance of things hoped for.

Look at faith as the tangible evidence of your dreams and aspirations. It's not merely about wishful thinking but is manifested through your actions. For instance, if you're planning a trip from London in England to Edinburgh in Scotland, faith is evident in the concrete steps you take, such as purchasing a train ticket, packing your bags, and arranging your travel itinerary, etc. Faith is about demonstrating through your preparations and actions that you're committed to realising your goals.

Being a leader in this context involves taking charge of your journey and leading yourself towards fulfilment. It's about believing in your vision and taking proactive steps to make it a reality. While it may be challenging to convince others to join you on your journey, it's essential to remain steadfast in your convictions and lead by example. People define you based on how they met you. So, don't allow how people define you or to limit who you are. You're much more than what people say or think. Regardless of seasonal changes, always preserve your purpose.

Vision gives you steady direction, purpose keeps you in check. Your mission is to fulfil your purpose and accomplish your vision.

Each one of us has the power to make our place matter. We can create a world filled with meaningful contributions. So, let us embrace our unique place in this world and strive to make a positive difference.

Self Reflections:

1. Reflect on a time when you felt most fulfilled in your life. What were you doing, and why did it bring you fulfilment? How does this experience align with your sense of purpose?

_____

_____

_____

_____

_____

2. Where do you struggle to stay aligned with your vision and purpose, and what steps can you take to improve in these areas?

_____

_____

_____

_____

3. Can you identify any concrete steps you've taken recently that demonstrate your commitment to make your place matter?

_____

_____

_____

_____

In this chapter, we've explored the profound interconnectedness of vision, dreams, and purpose in shaping our lives and driving us towards personal fulfilment and impact. From recognising our unique purpose to empowering our dreams and unveiling the driving force behind our actions, each element plays a crucial role in guiding our journey. Through examples of visionary leaders, we've witnessed the transformative power of aligning our actions with our deepest aspirations. As we embrace self-leadership and faith in our vision, we are empowered to navigate challenges and inspire positive change. Ultimately, the journey towards making our place matter is one of clarity, determination, and commitment to realising our dreams and fulfilling our purpose.

In the next chapter, let's explore overcoming barriers to fulfilling purpose. As we strive to make our place matter, it's crucial to address challenges head-on.

Chapter 7 Highlights

- Vision, dreams and purpose are three interconnected entities.

- To make your place matter, you need to do something that will matter.

- Without action or determination, dreams may remain as mere fantasies. Our gifts make us invaluable, not just to ourselves, but to the world.

- Effective leadership requires refining one's unique abilities and developing resilience to navigate complex and challenging situations.

Chapter 8

Overcoming Barriers to Fulfilling Your Purpose

"I think a hero is an ordinary individual who finds strength to persevere and endure in spite of overwhelming obstacles." **Christopher Reeve**

This Space; Your Place

Have you ever paused to consider the story of Biblical Joseph? It's a narrative that, when closely examined, reveals the power of a purpose-driven life, even when faced with the most formidable barriers. Joseph's life wasn't a walk through the park; it was a journey through storms and deserts. Yet, he emerged not only unscathed but victorious. Why? Because he understood that every obstacle was an opportunity in disguise – a chance to grow, to excel, to lead in his place of gifting.

In the pages of his life, we see a young man whose dreams were his compass, undeterred by betrayal or the cold walls of a foreign prison. He held onto his vision with unwavering faith, and this vision brought clarity, direction, and eventual ascendancy within a land that was not his own. It's the kind of story that fuels my belief that every one of us has a seed of greatness within, waiting to sprout amidst the adversities we encounter.

As we delve into this chapter, consider this: What are the 'prisons' you find yourself in? What dreams have you tucked away for 'someday'? I invite you to journey with me, to see these barriers not as dead-ends but as bends in the road, guiding us toward our ultimate purpose. Let's explore how to turn setbacks into setups, and predicaments into platforms for achievement. For in the Divine plan of life, it is not the obstacles we face but how we overcome them that defines our path to success.

As I reflect on the lives of the many people I've had the privilege to meet and mentor, one truth stands resolute: deep within, there's a universal yearning for peace and purpose. Yet, it's not merely about personal satisfaction; it's about finding one's place in the space of life, making a difference that is uniquely their own.

The journey to purpose is deeply personal, a solitary path walked in the company of your own convictions. It is not determined at birth, nor is it the result of serendipitous encounters alone. Instead, it's sculpted by the hands of your experiences, moulded by the decisions you make, and brought to life by the dreams you dare to chase. This journey is not without its obstacles; barriers will rise like ancient citadels, imposing and seemingly insurmountable.

> *The journey to purpose is deeply personal, a solitary path walked in the company of your own convictions.*

Yet, as we embark on this chapter together, remember that each barrier is a question posed to your spirit. Will you retreat, or will you rise? These challenges, whether cloaked in ambiguity or stark in their presence, are not the architects of your destiny – you are. It is in the overcoming, the relentless pursuit of 'what could be,' that we find the essence of purpose.

Purpose gives direction, a compass by which to chart your course. It lends meaning to your actions and empowers you to evolve into an individual of impact, an agent of change within your community, and indeed, within the world. Embracing your purpose can deliver you from the mires of confusion and place you firmly on the grounds of clarity.

We all have our reasons for rising each morning, our 'whys' that fuel our 'what's' and 'hows'. While I can share insights and guide you through the principles, the real journey begins with you. So, as we navigate the list of barriers, let us hold fast to the belief that each step taken is a step closer to the fulfilment that awaits us. Let's commit to this quest not just for ourselves, but for the generations that will follow, charting a course that turns today's dreams into tomorrow's realities.

Now, let's venture forth and discover how we can transform barriers into bridges, obstacles into opportunities, and dreams into destinies.

Overcoming Barriers to Fulfilling Your Purpose

1. Personal and Self-Imposed Barriers

Lack of clarity: One of the major barriers that I must highlight, is the lack of clarity. To possess clarity is to hold a steadfast understanding of your purpose, undeterred by the bustle around you or the pursuits of others. It's about having a recognition of your path, and let's not misinterpret this – clarity isn't a static state. It evolves, becoming sharper and more defined as you progress through life's journey. Initially, your vision might not be perfect, but it's vital to have that initial clarity as a starting point.

The absence of clarity is a formidable adversary in the quest for purpose. I remember teaching a live webinar on Zoom, focusing on the crucial topic of discovering one's purpose. As the session progressed, I posed a question to the attendees. "What do you aspire to achieve in the long run?" One attendee's response, which appeared in the chat box, simply read "anything." It was a single word, but it spoke volumes about the common barrier of lack of clarity that many face. Some express a desire to merely get by, to accept whatever comes their way, but such indistinctness is a roadblock. It's challenging for anyone to offer guidance when the direction is unknown. How can one provide support on a journey to fulfilment when the destination is a mystery? It is Zig Ziglar who once said, "If you aim at nothing, you will hit it every time."

People must comprehend the utmost importance of knowing – not just having a faint idea, but truly knowing with conviction – what they desire in life. Often, individuals are told they possess the capability to do various things, and while versatility is commendable, a person with a purpose will focus on what they are truly passionate about. You may have many gifts, and as you nurture them, you might discover the potential to branch out into other areas. However, this doesn't mean you should diverge from your chosen path.

Being clear about your goals enables you to streamline your journey. With clarity, you can see your path brightly lit, avoiding obstacles that may cause you to stumble. It grants you the pace and precision in your steps – you'll know where to tread and where to halt, whom to engage with and whom to avoid, which materials are essential and which resources are superfluous. Clarity ensures that you don't carry burdens that will slow your progress. It is not just important, but imperative, for clarity illuminates your way, allowing you to navigate life's journey with agility and assurance.

Inability to self-motivate and lead: In my journey of teaching leadership principles, I've observed a common hurdle that many aspiring individuals face – the challenge of self-motivation and the capacity to lead oneself. You see, leadership isn't just about guiding others; it's fundamentally about being the captain of your own ship first.

The very core of personal development is self-motivation. It's the spark that ignites the engine of our actions and the fuel that keeps it running. Yet, it is this inner drive that many find elusive. In the absence of it, even the most talented among us can find themselves adrift, unable to steer through life's waters with intention and purpose.

Now, if you find yourself in this predicament, where the drive to move forward is lacking, the solution isn't to look outward but to delve deeper within. It's about aligning your actions with your core values, finding your 'why', and letting that purpose be the beacon that guides you.

Begin by setting clear, achievable goals that resonate with what matters most to you. Break them down into small, actionable steps, and celebrate each milestone, no matter how small. This practice lays down a trail of successes that boost your confidence and stoke the fires of motivation.

Furthermore, develop a ritual of daily reflection and self-affirmation. Remind yourself of your strengths and past triumphs. Understand that leadership is not a title bestowed but a behaviour embraced. Each morning, ask yourself, "What is the one thing I am committed to leading in today?" Whether it is in thought, attitude, or action, be the leader of that commitment.

And remember, self-leadership is about discipline. It is about making the choice to do what you must do, even when you don't feel like doing it. Discipline is the bridge between goals and accomplishment, and self-motivation is the strong wind that carries you across that bridge. Be the leader you would follow, and soon, you'll not only inspire yourself but also become an inspiration to others.

> *Be the leader you would follow, and soon, you'll not only inspire yourself but also become an inspiration to others.*

Self-doubt and lack of self-confidence: Self-doubt is a barrier that lurks in the shadows of our minds, casting its gloomy haze on our brightest aspirations. I remember distinctly, back in 2008-2009, standing on the precipice of a major decision in my life. It was a turbulent time, with the economic crash sending shockwaves around the globe. And there I was, about to leap into the unknown.

Many of us face these junctures, where the steps we must take propel us into arenas we've never graced before. The uncertainty is palpable, the risk, intimidating. And yet, it is in these moments that our true resolve is tested. You see, it's not the certainty of success that should drive us, but the worthiness of the pursuit itself.

In those days, amidst the chaos, I made a choice. It wasn't just about taking a step, it was about taking ownership. Rather than looking to others to shoulder the blame for potential failure, I embraced responsibility. This mindset shift was pivotal. It's not about eradicating self-doubt – it's about confronting it, understanding it, and ultimately, mastering it.

If *your place* of purpose doesn't stretch you, if it doesn't make you a little uneasy, it's not audacious enough. Vision, by its nature, should be grand,

> *If your place of purpose doesn't stretch you, if it doesn't make you a little uneasy, it's not audacious enough.*

almost unnervingly so. If it doesn't make your heart skip a beat, then perhaps it's not a vision at all, but merely a dream.

And so, with clarity as my ally and courage in my pocket, I faced my fears. The steps I took weren't just in pursuit of success; they were strides towards understanding that there is nothing beyond the reach of a determined soul.

I often share this with my children and those I mentor: Seize every opportunity, no matter how daunting it may seem. Whether you're called upon to speak at a conference or to give an impromptu tribute at a gathering, let not self-doubt silence you. Step up, speak out, and in doing so, shatter the chains of fear.

You see, each word you utter, each action you take, carves a little more of your path. It's not about the applause at the end; it's about the growth within. By standing in the face of fear, by daring to be heard, you defy self-doubt. It's not just about building confidence; it's about cementing a foundation of resilience.

So, I urge you – when self-doubt whispers in your ear, answer with action. Turn your uncertainty into a clarion call for courage. Remember, it's not the absence of fear that defines us, but our response to it. Embrace the challenge, for it is the crucible in which the steel of your character is forged.

The fear of failure: Les Brown, a renowned motivational speaker once said, "Don't let the fear of failure overcome your

Overcoming Barriers to Fulfilling Your Purpose

desire to succeed." This is so true for many. They have lost their place in *this space* because of fear.

The fear of failure is not just about failing per se, but the fear of taking that initial leap. This trepidation isn't about failing; it's the fear of the unknown, the fear of venturing into uncharted territories – even if it's something you're deeply passionate about. The fear of the first step, of stepping into a new environment, is always there.

And let's not misconstrue failure. To put it into perspective, failure isn't about you as a person; it's about the task at hand not working out despite your efforts. You haven't failed if you haven't tried. You can't know the outcome without taking action. Therefore, the fear of failure is a grand deceit, a significant distraction that hinders the pursuit of one's purpose in life. Failure isn't final; it's a stepping stone towards greatness. Remember, every significant achievement starts small.

When you hesitate to take that first step into *your place*, fearing it won't measure up to the grand vision you have, remember that every journey begins with a single step. The fear of failure will taunt you with thoughts of wasted time and resources, of the challenges that lie ahead, and of the established names in the field.

But these fears are mere illusions; they hold no weight.

Consider this: those who are now established in the field didn't achieve overnight success; they may have been at it for decades. You are merely embarking on your own journey. Rather than succumbing to fear, let it be a source of strength. Embrace the understanding that they, too, likely faced failures and that these setbacks taught them valuable lessons. By not taking that step, you fail by default. But by taking it, you open the doors to learning and growth.

The bravery to take the first step is not a prelude to failure but an essential catalyst for progress. So let's recognise that the fear of failure is merely a barrier that must be confronted and overcome. We mustn't fear fear itself, for it is not the truth. It's akin to a wall that seeks to block your path; yet, if you have the courage to push against it, it will crumble, paving your way to greatness. In her book "Do It Afraid: Embracing Courage in the Face of Fear," Joyce Meyer explores the notion that fear is an inevitable part of life, but it doesn't have to dictate our actions. She encourages people to step out of their comfort zones and pursue their goals, even when they are afraid. The central message is that acting courageously often involves doing what we are afraid to do and that faith can be our guide in the face of fear. Do it afraid – that is how you will break this barrier!

Distractions that dilute focus: Distractions are ever present, vying for our attention and scattering our focus. They come in various guises, often masquerading as opportunities or obligations, yet they can easily lead us off the path of our true purpose.

In the journey of life, time is a commodity we cannot afford to squander. It moves with relentless momentum, never pausing, never waiting. Change is its constant companion, shifting the landscape around us with or without our consent. As leaders of our own lives, we must learn to adapt, to anticipate, and to continue our forward march.

I often tell people that it's not the number of hours that count, but the productivity within those hours. Imagine if every moment was an investment – would you spend it on distractions or on actions that lead to growth? It's essential to distinguish between movement and progress. A rocking horse keeps moving but makes no progress; we must aim

> *When you find yourself besieged by distractions, ask yourself: "Does this align with my place of purpose?"*

to be more like the thoroughbred, purposeful and directed.

Let's talk about handling these distractions. It's about prioritisation and understanding the difference between what is urgent and what is important. The urgent can often wait; the important should not. It's about setting boundaries and knowing when to say no. It's about having the discipline to stay true to your course when everything around you tempts you to veer off track.

When you find yourself besieged by distractions, ask yourself: "Does this align with my place of purpose? Will this take me closer to my goals?" If the answer is no, have the courage to let it pass by. Time and change will do what they inherently do – move forward. Our task is not to control them but to harness them, to make every tick of the clock count towards something meaningful.

Remember, the essence of leadership is not just about leading others; it's about leading yourself through the distractions and the changes, emerging not just unscathed, but stronger, more focused, and with greater clarity of vision. So hold fast to your goals, embrace the discipline required to achieve them, and you'll transform the very distractions that once hindered you into stepping stones towards your success.

2. Economic and Societal Barriers

Societal norms that dictate a specific path. Economic and societal barriers often stem from deep-rooted conventions and educational structures that guide us towards certain professions – be it medicine, engineering, law, or piloting. From a young age, we're nudged into these paths, sometimes without the opportunity to truly explore what resonates with our inner being. This can lead to a misalignment between our job and our true purpose, fostering a sense of frustration and stress rather than fulfilment.

The solution to navigating these societal expectations is not to dismiss them entirely but to approach them with discernment. It requires a conscious effort to unlearn the notion that success is a one-size-fits-all concept. Here's how we can start to address this barrier: Addressing the economic and societal barriers that shackle us to conventional career paths requires a thoughtful and deliberate process of introspection and action. To begin with, we must engage in self-reflection, allowing ourselves the space to discover our true talents and passions, understanding what truly motivates us beyond societal accolades. This process often involves re-evaluating our educational choices and career paths, seeking out fields of study or professional engagements that resonate with our core interests, even if they diverge from traditional expectations.

It's crucial to recognise that it's never too late to realign our careers with our passions. Whether it's through further education, taking up new courses, or embarking on side projects, these steps can pivot us towards a life that is more in tune with our inner calling. This shift requires a mindset that sees success as a personal journey rather than a universal standard. It also necessitates building a network of diverse individuals whose experiences and insights can illuminate the multitude of paths available to us.

Seeking mentorship can provide guidance and reassurance as we navigate new terrains, and developing emotional resilience will help us withstand the inevitable resistance that comes with change. Taking purposeful action, no matter how small, sets us on a trajectory towards our passions, gradually peeling away the layers of conventional success to reveal a career that is not just a job, but a reflection of our true selves. When we align our job with our innermost desires, we transform our relationship with work. Mondays cease to be a source of dread, instead becoming a welcome return to a meaningful, impactful engagement that we truly enjoy. It is in this alignment that we find a deeper happiness, a sense of fulfilment that elevates our everyday experiences and empowers us to soar to new heights.

Environmental Barriers: As I was scrolling on social media, I chanced upon a video. It featured a young Nigerian man, his voice filled with despair, declaring the sheer difficulty of succeeding in his homeland. He spoke of the overwhelming challenges – the economic struggles, the socio-political barriers – and he advised those who could, to leave the country in pursuit of opportunities somewhere else. This narrative, while grounded in real adversity, is not the whole story.

You see, within that same environment, there are young, vibrant individuals making waves globally. They have chosen not to let the barriers of their environment dictate their potential. They are testaments to the fact that while our surroundings can influence us, they do not have to define us.

This brings us to the critical discussion of environmental barriers. Whether it's the political climate, the economic landscape, our immediate family, or the country of our birth, these factors have undeniable potential to shape our journey. Many individuals facing such barriers may find themselves deviating from their intended path, their progress diverted by the circumstances they encounter.

Yet, let us not forget that a person driven by purpose, who is resolute in their pursuit of their passion, will carve a path through even the most stifling of environments. They understand that their purpose is not a product of circumstances but of determination and resilience.

A person of purpose does not see an impenetrable wall but challenges to navigate. Where some see a closed door, they find a window, a crack through which the light of opportunity shines. It's not merely about escaping one's environment but transforming it, about being a place of hope and progress that can inspire others.

In *this space* called life, it's the people who rise above their environment, who redefine the possible, that capture our imagination and admiration. They don't merely succeed despite their barriers; they do so because they have the vision to see beyond them. They embody the principle that our environment, no matter how challenging, should not be a prison but a canvas – and it is up to us, with bold strokes of courage and determination, to paint our masterpiece.

So to that young man, and to all who share his sentiment, I say this: do not let the environment be the end of your story. Let it be the beginning of a story of triumph, a narrative that speaks not of escape but of transformation. For in the heart of adversity lies the seed of greatness, waiting for the relentless spirit of human resolve to bring it to life. A person of purpose will always find a way out!

In the biblical account, Mephibosheth is the grandson of King Saul and the son of Jonathan. After the death of Saul and Jonathan, Mephibosheth's nurse fled with him to a place called Lo-debar, which was a remote area, cut off from the royal court where Mephibosheth might have been expected to live due to his royal lineage.

Despite these barriers, Mephibosheth's story does not end in Lo-debar. King David, honouring his covenant with Jonathan, seeks out Mephibosheth and restores to him the land of his grandfather Saul, and Mephibosheth eats at the king's table like one of the king's sons. This turn of events illustrates overcoming environmental barriers, where one's beginnings do not determine their end, and that recognition and opportunity can change one's course of life significantly.

This story teaches us the importance of not letting environmental factors dictate one's potential and the value of remaining open to opportunities that can lead to a breakthrough, much like Mephibosheth experienced when he was brought out of Lo-debar and into the king's palace.

Dwayne Johnson, famously known as 'The Rock,' had a challenging upbringing. He grew up in a family with a history of wrestling but faced adversity early in his life. At one point, his family struggled financially, and they were evicted from their apartment when he was a teenager. Additionally, he experienced multiple setbacks in his football career, including being cut from the Canadian Football League, which led him to reevaluate his path.

Despite these obstacles, The Rock persevered. He transitioned from football to professional wrestling, where his talent, charisma, and hard work led him to become one of the most iconic figures in the wrestling world. He later ventured into acting, where he faced skepticism about his ability to succeed beyond his wrestling persona. However, through dedication and relentless effort, he became a successful Hollywood actor, starring in blockbuster movies and establishing himself as one of the highest-paid actors in the industry.

The Rock's journey from adversity to success showcases

resilience and determination in the face of challenging environments. He didn't let his setbacks define him but instead used them as motivation to carve out a remarkable career in multiple fields. His story serves as an inspiration, illustrating how one can overcome environmental barriers through perseverance, hard work, and a relentless pursuit of goals.

3. Change of Circumstances

Setbacks and unforeseen circumstances: Delays and disappointments often emerge as formidable barriers on our life's journey. Such changes – a bereavement, the relocation of a close friend, or any event that disrupts our usual trajectory – can temporarily divert us from our path. However, it is essential for a person dedicated to their goals to gather themselves, reassess, and redefine their course of action. A setback might mean taking steps back, but the resolve to continue moving forward is a significant stride in the right direction. You will rebound in time.

Therefore, it is crucial not to place limits on yourself. Remember, you possess a remarkably creative and unfettered mind – dynamic, powerful, and full of purpose – that refuses to be constrained. Keep pushing ahead, undeterred by comparisons to others, which only serve to hinder your progress. Focus on your objectives and tirelessly work towards them. If your environment is less than ideal, take the initiative to forge your own path, paving the way to fulfilment and success.

In Dr. Spencer Johnson's book, 'Who Moved My Cheese?', we encounter four characters: two mice, Sniff and Scurry, and two miniature humans, Hem and Haw, who are all in a maze searching for their precious cheese. This cheese is more than just a food source to them; it symbolises the purpose, goals and desires we all chase after in life – be it career success, financial stability, or personal happiness.

One day, the cheese supply that Sniff, Scurry, Hem, and Haw had come to rely on disappears. This unforeseen circumstance tests each character's ability to adapt to change. The mice, without overthinking, immediately accept the loss and set off into the maze to find new cheese. They understand that change is a constant and adaptability is key to survival.

On the other hand, Hem and Haw react differently. They are stunned by the loss, feel victimised, and spend precious time denying and resisting change. Hem, in particular, refuses to leave the empty cheese station, paralysed by fear, while Haw eventually realises that he must overcome his fears and venture into the unknown to find new cheese.

This story serves as an exemplary metaphor for our discussion. Setbacks and unforeseen circumstances, like the disappearance of the cheese, are inevitable in life's maze. They can derail our plans and leave us feeling lost. However, it's not the setback itself that defines our journey; it's how we respond to it. Like the mice, we must not let fear or comfort in the familiar prevent us from seeking new opportunities. The courage to let go of old cheese and the pursuit of new cheese, despite the uncertainty it brings, is what propels us forward and enables us to adapt and grow.

So in the face of disruption or sudden change, remember the mice. Be swift to acknowledge the new reality, let go of the past, and move on to find new cheese, new opportunities, and new growth. This mindset, of embracing change as an opportunity rather than a barrier, is what separates those who thrive in *this space* from those who stagnate.

4. Resource Limitations

The perception of lacking resources: It is Tony Robbins who said, "It's not the lack of resources, it's your lack of resourcefulness that stops you." The essence of Robbins' statement is that external resources, while helpful, are not the deciding factor in whether someone can achieve their goals. Instead, it is a person's resourcefulness – their inner qualities and skills in making the most of whatever they have – that truly enables them to succeed. This perspective encourages individuals to shift their focus from what they lack to how they can creatively utilise their existing assets, skills, and opportunities to move forward.

Money, a resource we often deem as indispensable in our quest to fulfil our calling, may not be the primary requisite we've been led to believe it is. As we embark upon the path to our true purpose, we must re-evaluate the resources that truly matter.

The pursuit of one's life purpose is fundamentally driven by the wealth within – our innate talents, fervent passions, and the unique amalgamation of strengths that each of us possesses. It is this internal treasury that forms the bedrock of our purposeful voyage. One need not await the abundance of financial backing to commence their journey. The most impactful endeavours often sprout from humble origins – small, yet significant actions that serve as stepping stones towards a larger goal, devoid of substantial economic input. Scripture encourages us never to despise small beginnings.

Overcoming Barriers to Fulfilling Your Purpose

Resourcefulness transcends the mere availability of resources. It embodies the innovative spirit to utilise what is at hand in novel and effective ways. This creativity often carves paths where none seemed to exist and is a critical skill for anyone walking in purpose. The edifice of purpose is not constructed overnight. It is an edifice built brick by brick, experience by experience. Each stage of the journey allows for expansion and growth, often without the need for financial expenditure.

In the realm of purpose, relationships can prove to be more valuable than currency. Fostering a network of like-minded individuals can unlock doors to opportunities and collaborations, creating a multiplier effect on one's efforts.

> *In the realm of purpose, relationships can prove to be more valuable than currency. Fostering a network of like-minded individuals can unlock doors to opportunities and collaborations, creating a multiplier effect on one's efforts.*

In our modern age, the digital world offers an abundance of tools and platforms where one's purpose can flourish. Many of these resources are available at no cost, providing a fertile ground for ideas to grow and thrive.

Volunteering one's time and expertise is not only a noble

endeavour but also a powerful means of aligning with one's purpose. It is through such acts that we can gain invaluable experience, widen our perspective, and touch lives, all without a financial transaction.

Lack of support from people: In my experience as a coach and leader, I've encountered many individuals who lament their lack of support as they pursue their dreams. It's a common refrain, whether they speak of indifferent governments, unsupportive families, or friends who can't quite grasp their vision. But let's pause and consider this – does the absence of support truly halt our progress? I would maintain that it does not.

Oprah Winfrey's early life was marred by poverty and abuse. She was fired from her first job as a television reporter because she was 'unfit for TV.' Despite this lack of support, she went on to create her talk show, which became one of the most successful programmes in history.

What does this teach us? That the presence of support is a comfort, yes, but its absence is not a curse. It is, instead, an opportunity – an invitation – to delve into the depths of our resourcefulness. As leaders, as visionaries, we must cultivate a self-reliance that enables us to thrive even in the leanest of times.

Consider the present day, with its economic upheavals and global challenges. These are not the times to await aid but to act. I myself have turned to the earth, setting up a small family farm. It's a humble endeavour, but one that reconnects us to the fundamentals of life – sowing, nurturing, harvesting. And there's a metaphor here, isn't there? Just as we cultivate our land, we must cultivate our resolve, our self-sufficiency.

So, let us not cast blame for the support we lack. Instead, let us look within and around us and ask: How can I innovate? How can I adapt? Remember, no barrier, be it born of circumstance or scarcity, should ever be deemed powerful enough to detain us from our destined path. Your genesis does not define your journey's zenith. No dearth of support can impede a heart undeterred, a will unyielding. Forge ahead, and in doing so, you become the architect of your own destiny.

5. Comparison and External Validation

Comparing one's life with others: The act of comparing oneself to others is a deeply ingrained human tendency, often exacerbated by societal pressures and the pervasive influence of social media. However, this comparison can be a pernicious trap, leading to a never-ending cycle of dissatisfaction and a sense of inadequacy. It distracts us from the more vital and fulfilling journey of aligning our lives with our internal compass – what I refer to as the burden inside.

This inner burden is the seed of purpose that, when nurtured, defines who we are and guides us towards our unique contribution to the world. Unlike external comparisons, which are often about achieving more or appearing better than others, aligning with our inside burden is about authenticity and self-realisation.

There is a story about two neighbours who were caught up in a rather absurd contest – the Bed Wars. It all started when one showed off a splendid new four-poster bed. This stirred a sense of envy, comparison and competition in the other, who promptly responded by acquiring an even more elaborate bed. Thus began an unspoken rivalry, with each acquisition based not on need, but on outshining the other.

As the competition escalated, the beds became increasingly opulent, with one boasting a bed with built-in speakers and ambient lighting, and the other countering with a contraption that included a massage function and a fold-away home cinema. With each new upgrade, neighbours peeked through their curtains, gossiping about the spectacle of luxury being paraded onto their quiet street.

Overcoming Barriers to Fulfilling Your Purpose

It wasn't just about beds anymore; it was about status, about not being outdone by the house next door. The credit card bills piled up as they spent money they didn't have, to impress neighbours who watched with a mix of jealousy and amusement.

After the latest bed arrived, which seemed more like a spaceship than sleeping arrangement, complete with a control panel more complex than a car's dashboard, one of the neighbours stood in his bedroom. He sighed, a tinge of exhaustion beneath his amusement. "I can't even sleep anymore," he said to himself. "I'm up all night trying to figure out the controls for this thing."

And there it was, the irony of it all. They had accumulated debt to buy lavish furniture they didn't need, to impress neighbours they didn't even like, and now, the beds that were meant for restful slumber had become sources of sleepless nights. It was a powerful lesson, albeit learned the hard way – life is not a competition with your neighbour. Fulfilment can't be found in material possessions or in seeking validation through comparison. True contentment in *this space* comes from within, from living a life authentic to oneself, unmarred by societal pressures and the needless chase for human approval.

Identifying Barriers to Purpose Discovery: A Framework

Understanding our life's purpose is often obscured by barriers that can be both internal and external. Identifying these barriers is the first step towards overcoming them and moving closer to realising our true potential. Here's a straightforward framework to help you in this process:

1. **Self-Reflection**: Begin by asking yourself, "What did I always want? What would I prefer to have?" Write these aspirations down to create a tangible record of your desires.

2. **Barrier Recognition**: Examine why you are not currently in possession of what you desire. Write down the reasons that come to mind. These reasons are the barriers you face – acknowledging them is a crucial step in the journey of self-improvement.

3. **Strategy Development**: With your barriers identified, ask, "How do I deal with them?" Develop strategies to overcome each barrier, breaking them down into manageable steps. This could involve seeking out new skills, acquiring knowledge, or changing certain behaviours.

4. **Action Planning**: Create an action plan with specific,

time-bound goals. Commit to these actions with the understanding that they are the catalysts for change in your life's trajectory.

5. **Skill Enhancement**: If your barriers are related to a lack of competence in certain areas, commit to training and certification. Upgrading your skills will empower you to overcome professional and personal hurdles.

6. **Obligation Beyond Self**: Recognise that overcoming barriers may not just be for your own benefit but for those whose lives are connected to your purpose. Your progress could be the key to unlocking potential in others.

7. **Embrace the Journey**: Accept that barriers come in many forms, from colleagues who may not share your vision to systemic bureaucratic hurdles. Plan strategically and be prepared to push through with persistence.

Remember, the journey to discovering and fulfilling your purpose is not a solitary one. It's a path shared with others, and often, it's the lives we touch along the way that define the true measure of our success. Your journey may be for more than just your own fulfilment – it could be the beacon that guides others to their own purpose.

Chapter 8 Highlights

- Despite socioeconomic and political challenges, individuals can achieve notable success through resilience and an unwavering pursuit of their goals.

- Delays and disappointments may temporarily divert one's intended path, but dedication to one's objectives allows for recovery and continued advancement.

- It is a person's resourcefulness, rather than the amount of resources at hand, that is the decisive factor in achieving one's ambitions.

- The absence of external support does not prevent progress; self-reliance and internal fortitude can drive individuals towards success.

Chapter 9

The Role of Success and Fulfilment In Your Life

"Circumstances do not make a man, they reveal him."

Wayne Dyer

This Space; Your Place

As the applause dwindled following my presentation to some young leaders at a conference, I scanned the room, filled with the eager faces of the next generation. It was in this charged atmosphere that a hand shot up, cutting through the air with determined curiosity. The young man attached to the hand stood up; his name tag read 'Ethan', and his eyes were alight with the quest for understanding.

Ethan: Excuse me Dr. I have a question. Would you say you're successful?

Me: Yes, Ethan, I would.

Ethan: During your talk, you mentioned goals quite a bit. Why do you consider yourself successful? Have you achieved all your goals?

Me: Success is not only in the accomplishment of our end goals but also in our daily strides towards them. My definition of success includes making progress every single day towards my life's ultimate ambitions, whether they be in my career, relationships, or personal growth.

Ethan: But if success is about achieving goals, and you're still in pursuit, is it accurate to call yourself successful now?

The Role of Success and Fulfilment In Your Life

Me: Success is incremental, Ethan. It's about setting benchmarks along the way to your ultimate goal. Each achieved benchmark is a success in its own right. It's akin to climbing a mountain; reaching a base camp is a success, even though you haven't summited yet.

Ethan: So, every step forward counts as success?

Me: Absolutely. The decision to embark on a journey, the determination to continue, the resilience to overcome setbacks – they're all significant achievements. As a student, for example, each exam you pass and every project you complete successfully brings you closer to graduation – each is a success.

Ethan: It's reassuring to hear that the journey matters as much as the destination.

Me: Indeed, it does. Success is about the journey and appreciating every step. The very act of planning and setting out on your path is a success. For example, today, I consider this dialogue we're having as a successful outcome of my presentation.

Ethan: That puts a lot of things into perspective. Thank you for addressing my question.

Ethan sat down, his question answered, but the spark in his eye told me that a new journey was just beginning for him. As the session continued, I reflected on the power of every small victory and the countless unseen successes that pave the way to our purpose.

Throughout history, numerous individuals have scaled the heights of wealth and fame, yet have grappled with feelings of inadequacy and perceptions of failure. Their outward triumphs, paradoxically, often belied an inner turmoil and discontent.

Take Marilyn Monroe, for instance. As a luminous icon of the silver screen, her name became synonymous with glamour and success in the mid-20th century. Despite the adoration of millions and a career that many would envy, Monroe's private life was shadowed by depression, anxiety and a persistent sense of isolation. The revelations from her diaries and personal correspondence paint a picture of a woman engaged in profound introspection, wrestling with the gnawing feeling that her true desires and aspirations remained unfulfilled.

This contradiction prompts the question: Why do some individuals feel unsuccessful despite appearances that suggest the contrary? The root of this conundrum often lies in the dissonance between society's conventional metrics of success – fame, fortune, acclaim – and the individual's personal benchmarks, which may encompass emotional well-being, authentic relationships, creative satisfaction, or a sense of purpose. For many, like Monroe, the societal accolade was not aligned with a personal definition of success, leading to an inner void that no amount of external validation could fill.

In examining such lives, we are reminded that 'success' is not a one-size-fits-all concept. It is a deeply personal construct that, when incongruent with an individual's core values and purpose, can render even the most enviable achievements hollow. The true measure of success, then, may not lie in the applause of the crowd but in the quiet fulfilment of one's own heart.

What is Success?

Defining success is often a subjective venture, as its essence varies from person to person. At its core, success can be described as the achievement of a set task, coupled with a sense of satisfaction with the outcome. It is not merely about completing a mission, but also about the joy and contentment that come with its fulfillment.

Success is the sum of small steps, repeated day in and day out.

In essence, success is episodic; it's an experience that is savoured in the moment. It signifies the culmination of one endeavour and, often, the initiation of another, more challenging one. Success is about progression, not just about reaching a destination. It ensures that one is engaged in a continuous process towards achieving a desired outcome, adhering to a path that leads to the realisation of a worthwhile goal.

Success, then, can be seen as a path rather than a definitive endpoint. It's about navigating through various stages or segments of achievement. The true beauty of success lies in its ability to propel us forward, to encourage us to delve deeper into our pursuits, and to strive for greater heights.

> *Success is the sum of small steps, repeated day in and day out.*

However, it's critical to distinguish between professional success and personal fulfilment. One can achieve considerable success in their career or a particular venture and yet feel a disconnect from the joy or fulfilment that one anticipates from such achievements. Thus, while success in one's career is commendable, it does not necessarily equate to overall happiness. The real triumph lies in aligning our successes with what truly brings us joy and contentment in life.

Success is indeed valuable, but fulfilment is significantly superior. Not every success leads to fulfilment, yet there is no fulfilment without some measure of success. There's nothing inherently wrong with success; it's highly esteemed and sought after universally. Success is what's seen; it shapes how people relate to and respond to you.

On the other hand, fulfilment is deeply personal, a kind of inner metric gauged by an intrinsic joy – a sentiment only you can truly articulate. Often, fulfilment may go unnoticed or uncelebrated; it doesn't typically result in awards or nominations. It may be a path trodden in solitude, but it's one where you feel content, proud, and profoundly thankful.

Fulfilment is comparable to the concept of not gaining the whole world at the expense of one's soul. What benefit is there in acquiring everything if it means losing what truly satisfies your soul?

What is Fulfilment?

This is not an attempt to differentiate or juxtapose success and fulfilment fundamentally, but rather to illuminate the nature, importance, and benefits of your pursuit – understanding the essence of existence.

Fulfilment is much deeper than success. One can be successful without feeling fulfilled, but fulfilment inherently includes some form of success. Fulfilment occurs when you achieve what truly resonates with your purpose – often described as that which brings you inner happiness. I'm not referring to ephemeral pleasures such as money, positions, accolades, titles, or awards. These might bring temporary happiness, but not necessarily fulfilment.

> *Fulfilment is much deeper than success. One can be successful without feeling fulfilled, but fulfilment inherently includes some form of success.*

True fulfilment could be something as simple as assisting someone in need, knowing that your help made a significant difference in their life. Such an act could bring you more fulfilment than possessing the wealth of the richest person on Earth. Being the richest person might garner titles and public recognition, but does it resonate with what truly matters to you? A high-flying career professional might reach the pinnacle of an organisation and be deemed successful, but whether they are

The Role of Success and Fulfilment In Your Life

fulfilled is a separate question entirely. It's not the promotions or the prestigious office that fulfil you. They might make you successful, recognised for your intellect, skills, and experience, but if stripped of these, would you still feel content and fulfilled?

This conundrum is evident when we see individuals with wealth, position, and seemingly perfect lifestyles still succumb to despair, evidenced by unconventional exits from life, such as suicide. Without delving into the specifics of each case, it's clear that the absence of fulfilment is a profound issue.

Fulfilment comes when you do what you truly desire. For some, success is a means to an end – a way to utilise resources to pursue what will ultimately lead to fulfilment. For instance, a person might use their earnings not as an end goal but as a tool to engage in endeavours that bring genuine satisfaction.

Therefore, while success is commendable, fulfilment is vastly superior. Not every successful endeavour leads to fulfilment, but there is no fulfilment without some measure of success. What defines success for you? It's a subjective measure. We all aim for greater success, continually striving for more. If you question your success, consider what standards you're using to judge it. Success is not universally defined; it's individual, based on the goals you set for yourself and the satisfaction derived from achieving them. Success is journey and fulfilment is a destination.

Failure is succeeding at the wrong thing. You may achieve success in something that isn't rightly considered a success, which can make you a miserable successful person. For example, a renowned English Premiership footballer was once asked what made him so successful in the game, and how he played it so beautifully that caught the attention of top football clubs and coaches worldwide. His answer was somewhat shocking; he confessed that he didn't really love football, nor did he watch it. He only did it for the job, knowing how to perform well. He said football didn't make him happy; it simply paid his bills. He questioned if anyone is truly a fan of the company they work for. The fame and awards other players coveted, of which he had many, did not excite him. His vision was not to be a professional athlete.

This also reminds me of the great tennis champion Nick Kyrgios, known for his prodigious talent. Nick struggled with the challenges that came with wealth, fame, and the labels imposed on him in the game – these were not for him. He decided to leave the game and fame for what brings him inner joy and ultimate fulfillment. Those labels did not adequately represent what he wanted to be known or remembered for.

The story of Jacob, a biblical figure, serves as a compelling illustration of the concept of fulfilment beyond material success. Jacob, who initially fled to his uncle Laban as a fugitive, eventually amassed great wealth, including flocks and servants, becoming one of the richest men in his region. Yet, there came a point when Jacob sought more than just possessions; he yearned for a deeper meaning in life.

This yearning, birthed from his earlier transformative moment when, resting his head upon a stone, Jacob experienced a profound dream, gnawed at him, leaving him unfulfilled despite his escapade at his uncle's house. This dream eventually propelled his escape from the servitude of ephemeral success to one that assured lasting peace and fulfillment. His escape led to a deeper turmoil inside; one that exposed his fear and helplessness. It was at this juncture he sought God's blessing, not in the form of additional wealth, but as a revelation of his true purpose.

The divine encounter marked a pivotal shift in Jacob's life; his name was changed to Israel, symbolising a new phase of existence that transcended material accumulation. Jacob's fulfilment was no longer tied to his possessions but to his identity and purpose. The renaming from Jacob to Israel represented a passage from mere existence to truly living.

Jacob's subsequent actions, such as seeking reconciliation with his estranged brother Esau, were steps toward liberation. True fulfilment allowed Jacob to walk with freedom, unconcerned with the need for defences or shields that typically protect one's earthly gains. He approached his brother not as a man boasting of his success but as one seeking genuine peace and resolution.

The narrative of Jacob teaches us that while success can offer protection and comfort, it is often shrouded with the need for constant safeguarding. In contrast, fulfilment transcends the superficial and aligns with our deepest sense of self and purpose. It is this state of fulfilment that Jacob ultimately achieved, illustrating that true peace comes from within and not from the abundance of possessions.

Creating the Right Mindset for Success

How can we avoid constructing incorrect notions of success in our minds?

The quote by Norman Vincent Peale, "Change your thoughts

and you change your world," speaks to the profound impact of our mindset on our experience of reality. In terms of creating a mindset of success, this statement suggests that our thought patterns are not just passive reflections of our circumstances, but active creators of our life's trajectory.

To foster the appropriate mindset for success, one must discern how to avoid the trap of comparing oneself to external, often unrealistic standards that can induce frustration. This frustration arises when one attempts to meet these external benchmarks that are neither self-created nor truly reflective of personal success. When individuals strive to emulate a fabricated image of success, they are setting themselves up for disappointment, as these ideals are frequently unattainable. Social media has made this more prominent.

> *To foster the appropriate mindset for success, one must discern how to avoid the trap of comparing oneself to external, often unrealistic standards that can induce frustration.*

The key to circumventing this pitfall is to sit down and define what success means to you personally. What milestones do you wish to achieve in your life that will make you feel successful? The metrics for measuring success are unique to each individual and are determined by the goals they set for themselves.

Consider the scenario of graduation: someone who graduates at twenty-five is no less successful than one who graduates at twenty-one. Success in this case is not about age, but about achieving the goal of graduation. And what about those who have never attended university but find success in business? They may end up employing university graduates, challenging the notion that formal education is the sole path to success.

Success is subjective. It's what you define for yourself. A graduate is successful because they've reached their personal goal, just as an entrepreneur who has built a business through apprenticeship and hands-on experience is successful in his own right.

The essence lies in defining your path and staying disciplined enough to focus on it. By simply being here, having overcome obstacles, you are successful. Embarking on a journey that you have charted for yourself, and persistently moving towards your chosen destination, is a success.

You are successful if you can set your goals, pursue them with intent, and achieve them. No one else should dictate what success looks like for you. As long as you're ticking the boxes of your

The Role of Success and Fulfilment In Your Life

personal checklist, whether it's a daily routine or long term objectives, you are achieving success. Let me encourage you that the 'success' you are chasing is already in you. You are a success! It's now your turn to speak it, believe it and act like a success!

Chapter 9 Highlights

- Success is a subjective concept, and is defined as making consistent progress towards one's life ambitions, rather than just the final achievement of those goals.

- The journey towards success is incremental, with each step forward and every benchmark achieved representing a form of success.

- True success should be aligned with personal fulfilment, which is deeply individual and goes beyond societal measures like wealth or fame.

- Fulfilment is the deeper pursuit within success, found in actions and achievements that resonate with one's inner purpose and happiness.

Chapter 10

Turning Challenges Into Opportunities

"I don't know what your destiny will be, but one thing I know: the only ones among you who will be really happy are those who have sought and found how to serve."

Albert Schweitzer

Every challenge carries the seed of equal or greater opportunity. This is a truth that, though often veiled by the immediate stress and discomfort of adversity, holds the promise of personal growth and purpose discovery.

Consider a tree that stands in the midst of a storm. Winds howl and the ground shakes, yet come dawn, it stands taller, roots entrenched more deeply into the fertile earth. Similarly, when we face our own tempests, the truest test isn't in the ferocity of the winds but in the depth of our resolve.

In *this space*, challenges are intricately woven threads that add depth and texture to our existence. They are not mere interruptions to our story but essential chapters that shape the narrative of who we become. When we view our hurdles not as impenetrable walls but as hurdles to leap over, we shift from being passive observers of our lives to active participants in a thrilling quest for excellence.

Growth is an incremental process, often invisible to the eye, and it is in the furnace of life's challenges that this growth is accelerated. Each obstacle overcome, each barrier breached, and each limitation transcended carves out a part of us that was previously undiscovered. It is through these challenges that we

Turning Challenges Into Opportunities

often stumble upon our life's calling, finding purpose in places we least expected.

The mindset that transforms challenges into opportunities is one of resilience and adaptability. It asks of us to not just endure but to engage – to not just survive but to thrive. It's about embracing the unknown and finding comfort in discomfort, knowing that the alchemy of personal transformation is at work.

In the pursuit of turning our trials into triumphs, it's essential to remember that our attitudes are the brushstrokes that colour our experiences. A perspective that looks for lessons in defeat, that finds strength in vulnerability, and sees the potential for renewal in every setback, is the kind of mindset that crafts a life of meaning and fulfilment.

I am inspired by the story of Nick Vujicic who was born without limbs, his journey began with immense obstacles that could have hindered any hope for a fulfilling life. Yet, Nick chose to embrace his situation with courage and determination.

As a child, Nick struggled with the emotional turmoil of feeling different. The challenge of a life without limbs was, at first, a dark cloud overshadowing his existence. But rather than let despair take hold, Nick discovered his innate ability to inspire others. He turned his unique life experience into a catalyst for change, becoming a renowned motivational speaker and touching the lives of millions.

Nick's story teaches us that our challenges, no matter how severe, can become gateways to growth and purpose. His example encourages us to look beyond our limitations and to see the potential for transformation. Each obstacle, then, becomes not just a barrier but a chance to innovate and to redefine what's possible.

The perception of obstacles as insurmountable barriers is a common misconception. In the realm of sales, for instance, what are often deemed as 'smoke objections' present themselves as real and intimidating, designed to thwart progress or prevent a sale. However, once these challenges are faced head-on, we typically discover that they were not as formidable as they appeared.

Take the journey through higher education as an example. The thought of undertaking a three or four-year degree can seem overwhelming at the outset. The first year is often the hardest, filled with academic challenges, stringent professors, and personal adjustments that can seem to conspire against your academic success. Yet, these challenges are not necessarily indicative of your

Turning Challenges Into Opportunities

inability to succeed but are rather tests of your perseverance.

What is most telling about these challenges is that they tend to vanish when you stop pushing forward, suggesting that their true purpose is to impede your progress. Recognising this can be a powerful motivator. When you encounter difficulties on your path to progress, they can serve as indicators that you are pursuing something meaningful and significant.

Challenges are a part of life's journey, and they differ for everyone. We all face varied trials and possess different levels of tolerance, self-control, and capabilities, not to mention varying degrees of support. While some may navigate these challenges with ease, others may need to draw upon deeper reserves of strength.

Moving forward and reaching for new levels of achievement will invariably involve encountering new challenges. These are the hurdles we must overcome as we journey to the next level of our personal or professional lives. They are not just obstacles but milestones marking our path to greater and higher achievements.

> *Moving forward and reaching for new levels of achievement will invariably involve encountering new challenges.*

Created To Confront Challenges

We are, fundamentally, beings engineered to confront and resolve problems. It has been suggested that the human brain is designed not only for success but also for survival. And on that note, survival itself is a form of success. We're not solely crafted to achieve, but also to withstand and endure the unexpected trials that life throws our way. The instinct to survive is embedded within each of us. How did we arrive at this point? It is through survival. Consider the biological process of conception: thousands of sperm vie for fertilisation, yet here you are, having triumphed in that very first challenge. From the moment of birth, we face and conquer obstacles – that in itself is success.

We are created to engage with challenges, to overcome obstacles, and to push forward with momentum and progress. We are not meant to be static or to be held back; we are fashioned for advancement and for movement. Therefore, no obstacle should be so daunting as to halt our journey.

However, it must be acknowledged that some individuals perceive challenges as overwhelming, allowing them to hinder progress and keep them subdued. Recognising that one can rise above obstacles, extract lessons from challenges, and reap benefits

Turning Challenges Into Opportunities

from failures or mistakes is essential for success in life. Do not shy away from the challenges that arise; instead, confront them with courage and resolve.

The satisfaction gained from overcoming a challenge is immense, instilling a sense of pride and accomplishment. At every stage of life, we encounter our own realities and the challenges inherent within them. Whether we aspire to reach higher echelons or remain in our current station, we are destined to face hurdles.

Life's journey is marked by stages: the challenges of the past, the struggles of the present, the difficulties of the season, and the uncertainties of the future. Each stage comes with its own set of obstacles. You are here today because you have already navigated the challenges of yesteryear. Think of the hurdles you've crossed as a child, a teenager, an adult, and now as you approach retirement and the later years. How did you persevere through these times?

There are two inexorable components in every person's life: time and change. These elements will manifest themselves to everyone, at different or similar seasons. Your approach to these moments, your mindset in the face of time, and your reaction to change, are the cumulative expressions of your character and purpose. How you respond to the passage of time and adapt to change defines your journey and shapes your destiny.

Problems Are Never Permanent

Challenges, as formidable as they may seem, are not indelible marks upon our lives. They have the potential to either break us or fortify us, depending on our mindset, our perception, and our resilience. While challenges can indeed halt progress and feel like insurmountable barriers, they also present a remarkable opportunity to catapult us into realms of personal greatness. They can unveil new strengths within us, unearth latent skills, and teach us novel approaches to life's complexities. No problem in your life is permanent.

Challenges, when embraced and transformed, can stimulate growth, foster critical thinking, and build a robust resilience that places us in an advantageous position for the future – a future where we grow into our full potential and fulfilment. Plato, the philosopher, encapsulated this when he said, "It takes guts to win." It's a testament to the notion that pursuing a greater purpose or goal in life is often accompanied by formidable challenges.

It's crucial to recognise that challenges are not permanent fixtures in our lives. They are transient, situational, and seasonal by nature. They come and go, but our core values, desires, and aspirations persist. Do not let today's difficulties steal away the prospects and rewards of tomorrow. Sometimes, pain is a necessary precursor to gain. Just as a medical injection may cause momentary discomfort, it is the medicine we require for healing. If we focus solely on the pain, we risk missing out on the treatment that restores our wellbeing.

> *It's crucial to recognise that challenges are not permanent fixtures in our lives. They are transient, situational, and seasonal by nature.*

Consider the joy and fulfilment that come with birthing a new life; it far outweighs the labour pains. Be patient with yourself, but also ensure that you are progressing, even if it's incrementally. Each small step is a step towards mastery. Your time will come, and your struggles will become the testament to your perseverance.

There is a profound beauty in this struggle; it is the crucible in which your purpose is refined and defined. Embrace it, and birth your purpose despite the adversities.

Moreover, the presence of challenges serves as a measure of the quality and magnitude of your purpose. If you surrender at the first sign of difficulty, perhaps your aspirations were not as grand as you thought. When faced with an obstacle, seek a pathway through it – find your freedom and truly be free.

In essence, the challenges we face are not just obstacles but also tests – tests that determine the strength of our commitment to our aspirations. The ability to navigate through these challenges is what can lead us to true deliverance and fulfilment.

Let us go forth, not just hoping for easier paths, but also as individuals fortified by our trials, empowered to turn every challenge into a stepping stone towards our grandest aspirations. It is in this endeavour that our greatest potential is realised and our true purpose is found.

See It Before You See It

The power of visualisation, or 'seeing it before you see it,' lies in the human mind's remarkable ability to simulate experiences and outcomes before they occur. This mental rehearsal is not just fanciful daydreaming; it's a potent tool that can shape our reality.

How can you explain or describe the inner feelings or sense of accomplishment that you experience when you have just overcome a challenge in your life? Can you articulate the emotions, the inner joy, and the outward radiance? These feelings drive you towards the next action, and the results you achieve will also enable you to draw strength from past victories to face new challenges as they arise. Just because you have overcome obstacles or 'crosswalks' successfully in your race to victory does not mean you won't encounter further hurdles before reaching the finish line. If you've managed to cross the first few, you're certainly capable of crossing the next ones, time and time again, on your path.

Another perspective, as rightly put by John C Maxwell, is that there is something beautiful about a challenge that brings the best out of us. Show me a person without challenges, and I'll show you someone who is living within their comfort zone. Indeed, the person truly challenged has a hill to climb and is willing to undertake the strenuous effort. It's a long and tough climb, but once you reach the top of the hill, the feeling is incredible. You'll be so glad you made the climb. Facing a challenge on your journey to fulfilment is a sign that you're drawing closer to the finish line, where victory or fulfilment awaits you.

The Divine Promise of Completion

If you approach life from a faith basis, I want you to see the journey of overcoming challenges and finding *your place* in the light of divine purpose and guidance. The Scripture assures us that, He who began a good work in you will complete it! This is a great source of encouragement to know that there is divine assistance on your journey to purpose.

This passage speaks to the steadfastness of God's work within us. It serves as a reminder that our lives are not a series of random events but are under the watchful eye of a Creator who is invested in our journey. When we face challenges, it's not merely our own strength we rely on; there is a deeper power at work, shaping us and guiding us towards a promised completion.

> *The challenges we encounter are not roadblocks meant to deter us, but rather they are tools used to sculpt our character, hone our strengths, and lead us to a place of intended fulfilment.*

In the context of personal growth and success, this belief translates into a confident assurance that our efforts are not in vain. The challenges we encounter are not roadblocks meant to deter us, but rather they are tools used to sculpt our character, hone our strengths, and lead us to a place of intended fulfilment.

For the faithful, every setback is an opportunity to witness the unfolding of a bigger plan. It's an invitation to lean into faith, to trust that the same force that initiated our path will also see us through to its completion. This is not a passive waiting but an active participation in a journey that is both personal and divinely orchestrated.

So, as you encounter each obstacle, remember that you are not alone. Your faith is not just a source of comfort; it is a call to action. It urges you to persevere, to press on, and to do so with the conviction that the outcome, though perhaps unseen, is assured by the faithfulness of the One who called you. With this in mind, view your challenges as milestones, markers of growth, and proof that the work within you is vibrant and ongoing.

Strategies for Overcoming Life's Challenges

Challenges are an integral part of life, shaping our personal narratives and the world around us. From individual hurdles to global upheavals, each challenge invites us to adapt, overcome, and emerge stronger. In this section, we explore practical strategies for navigating life's obstacles, embracing the notion that every problem holds the seed of growth and opportunity. We will discuss goal setting, decision-making, and the power of resilience, offering a blueprint for not just facing, but also harnessing the challenges that life presents. Prepare to engage with your challenges, transform them into stepping stones, and lead a life marked by growth and purpose.

1. **Understanding Personal Identity:** To conquer life's challenges, begin with self-discovery. Delve deeply into your own identity, values, and passions. Ask yourself critical questions: Who are you at your core? What are your unique talents and desires? What would you love to do if all constraints were removed? This introspection is the cornerstone of resilience and paves the way for authentic goal setting. People define you based on how they meet you. So, don't allow how people define you to limit who you are. You're much more than what people say or think. Regardless of seasonal changes, always preserve your purpose.

2. **Goal Setting:** Once you know yourself, define what you want to achieve. Set goals that resonate with your identity and passions. These goals should be clear, attainable, and

inspiring. Planning is essential; determine what is required to achieve your objectives, where to find the necessary resources, and outline the steps you need to take.

3. **Decision Making with Courage:** Goals require commitment. Decide with courage and conviction which paths you'll pursue. This decisive mindset is critical as it transforms intention into action. Courage doesn't mean the absence of fear, but rather the determination to move forward despite it.

4. **Focusing on Small Steps:** The journey toward your goals is a series of steps. Big aspirations can seem daunting, but breaking them down into smaller, manageable actions makes them achievable. Focus on each step, each day, each moment. This approach keeps you grounded and ensures steady progress.

5. **Seeking Support and Networking:** No one succeeds alone. Identify and engage with a community that aligns with your goals. Network with those who can offer support, advice, or resources. This network can become a powerful catalyst for overcoming obstacles and opening doors to opportunities.

6. **Adapting to Change:** Change is a constant, and adaptability is a key to resilience. Whether facing technological shifts, economic changes, or personal transitions, be prepared to pivot and adjust your strategies. Embrace change as an opportunity for growth.

7. **Maintaining Focus and Minimising Distractions:** Distractions are abundant; they can derail even the most determined individuals. Maintain a laser focus on your main goals and systematically reduce distractions. Keep your energy and attention on what truly matters for your success.

8. **Embracing Side Hustles Wisely:** Side hustles can provide valuable skills and financial support, but they should not overshadow your primary ambitions. Approach them as learning opportunities and stepping stones that complement your main pursuits.

9. **Self-Discipline:** Discipline is the bridge between goals and accomplishment. Cultivate self-discipline to persist in your endeavours. This means setting routines, holding yourself accountable, and staying true to your commitments.

10. **Willpower:** Willpower is the inner strength that propels you forward. Summon the will to progress, especially when faced with adversity. Your inner will is a renewable resource that grows stronger with use.

11. **Ignoring Negative Opinions:** On your path, you will encounter skepticism and criticism. Learn to filter out negative opinions that do not serve your purpose. Trust in your journey and the wisdom of your choices.

12. **Utilising Past Experiences:** Your past experiences are not mere memories; they are lessons. Leverage your history as a foundation for overcoming current and future obstacles. Each experience has shaped you and equipped you with knowledge for your journey.

13. **Keeping the Bigger Picture in Mind:** Never lose sight of the larger impact of your achievements. Remember the individuals who await the fruits of your labour, those whose lives you'll touch and inspire. Your success is not just for you – it's for the collective joy and advancement of others.

Chapter 10 Highlights

- Life's challenges, from personal issues to global crises, are inevitable and shape our existence.

- Each challenge is an opportunity for adaptation, growth, and increased strength. View your challenges as indicators of growth, and proof that the work within you is vibrant and ongoing.

- It's important to recognise that challenges are never permanent in our lives. They are momentary, and situational.

- A proactive approach to challenges, will turn them into catalysts for growth and meaningful living.

Chapter 11

The Importance of Starting Afresh

"No matter how small you start, start something that matters." **Brendon Burchard**

This Space; Your Place

As I approached my next birthday, I embarked on a new chapter, not just of life but in my life's work. This wasn't another academic paper or seminar presentation, this was the realisation of a personal ambition – my very own book,

My career had been full of accolades, my name associated with respected scholarly work. Yet, the dream to be an author, to hold a book that bore my name, had remained just that – a dream. It was a dream I nurtured quietly, waiting for its time.

This is my statement to the world, and more importantly, to myself: our aspirations have no sell-by date. This book – the first of many, is a witness to the belief that any moment is ripe for pursuit, for transformation, for seizing the pen and writing our own story.

This milestone wasn't merely about looking back with nostalgia; it was about stepping forward with renewed vigour. My book stands as evidence that the fulfilment of a dream knows no age, and that with each new page, we can continue to craft a narrative that resonates with passion and purpose.

It's imperative to start afresh if you're to fulfil your purpose, particularly if you've realised you've been 'rocking and rolling' on the wrong path – one that leads to dissatisfaction. It doesn't matter how far you've gone off course; the thrill of steering onto the right route toward your desired destination is exhilarating. That surge of happiness, that sense of being where you're meant to be, is something profoundly personal, a joy that only you can fully articulate.

However, the pain of journeying down a wrong path, one that is clearly not leading to your expected end, no matter the distance travelled, pales in comparison to the feeling of fulfilment that awaits if you would just turn back and start anew on the right course. This is the only way to reach your destination – to begin again.

The Pain of Unfulfilled Purpose

In the realm of unspoken desires and silent regrets, lies a profound anguish that resonates through the corridors of time. The hushed whispers of undiscovered destines, unutilised gifts and untapped potential. You will hate to die knowing that you have not done or completed what you're called for.

A dear friend of mine shared with me poignant moments, he experienced when he used to serve as a dentist in domiciliary settings. He took care of elderly residents in care homes and hospices. He had the opportunity to always strike a conversation with them and talk about their life stories. As he made his rounds, tending to the oral health of the elderly denizens, he often posed a simple yet profound question: "Do you have any regrets in life?"

For some of them, their responses, like echoes from a forgotten past, unveiled a common thread of yearnings – simple yet profound desires that time had gently tucked away. "I wish I had written a poetry book," one voice trembled with the weight of unwritten poetry. Another elderly resident when asked said, "When I was 32, I had an opportunity to work with a charity in Uganda, but I didn't take it. I was afraid. I don't even know what I was afraid of. I still wish I had gone there, to make a contribution to the lives of others," she sighed, her words carrying the burden of distant shores unexplored.

It was in their eyes, those windows to a lifetime of experiences, where the true narrative resided. A chorus of unspoken emotions lingered within their gaze – a vivid sense of remorse, and the sad melody of opportunities lost. The pain of unfulfilled purpose whispered through their words, painting a portrait of lives yearning to be lived to the fullest. Each syllable carried the weight of dreams deferred, aspirations unmet, and adventures yet to be undertaken. Their voices became a pitiful symphony of 'what ifs' and 'could have beens,' a silent plea to the living to not let their dreams wither away.

Some of their stories, told through veiled regrets and unfulfilled wishes, served as solemn reminders. They entreat us, the living, to seize the day, to pursue our passions, and to inscribe the pages of our lives with the ink of purpose and significance in *this space*.

The pain of unfulfilled purpose stands as an eloquent call – a timeless reminder to embrace aspirations, chase dreams, and script the chapters of life with fervour before the sun sets on our narratives. Their silent cries echo through time, urging us to heed the call of destiny before our own whispers join theirs in the corridors of time.

Why It's Never Too Late to Discover Purpose

Many people believe that finding their purpose in life is something they should have accomplished when they were young. They may feel they've

> *Discovering your purpose in life is not a one-time event but a continuous process that can happen at any stage of your life.*

missed their chance to pursue their true calling or that they're too old to make meaningful changes in their lives. However, this is not true. Discovering your purpose in life is not a one-time event but a continuous process that can happen at any stage of your life. Here are some reasons why it's never too late to discover your purpose:

You can always learn something new. Finding your purpose can inspire you to learn new skills, explore new interests, or develop new talents. Learning something new enriches your life, challenges your mind, and expands your horizons. You don't have to limit yourself to what you already know or do; there are always new possibilities and opportunities for growth and fulfilment.

You can always make a difference. Discovering your purpose can motivate you to make a positive impact on the world. You can use your gifts, passions, and values to serve others, contribute to a cause, or create something meaningful. You don't have to wait for the perfect moment or opportunity to make a difference; there are always ways to use your purpose to improve the world.

You can always find joy. Finding your purpose can bring you joy and happiness. When you live your purpose, you align your actions with your essence and express your true self. You don't

The Importance of Starting Afresh

have to settle for a life that's boring, unfulfilling, or meaningless; there's always joy in living your purpose and sharing it with others.

It allows you to redefine your purpose and rediscover yourself. It surely guides you toward your destination – ultimate fulfilment and happiness. What joy there is in being on the right path, doing what you've always desired, and finding true happiness in it. Your impact will be profoundly significant.

When it comes to the question of *your place* in *this space*, nothing is too late. As long as you are still here, you have the opportunity to start anew. You can discover or rediscover yourself; you can reinvent and redirect the course of your journey; you can make a U-turn, or a direct opposite turn, the moment you realise you are on the wrong path in life – and that can happen at any stage or age.

Let this quote inspire you in your journey. "Progress means getting nearer to the place you want to be. And if you have taken a wrong turn, then to go forward does not get you any nearer. If you are on the wrong road, progress means doing an about-turn and walking back to the right road; and in that case the man who turns back soonest is the most progressive man." – C.S. Lewis

You may have tried many different things in search of purpose;

there could be many ways or options open before you, but there is only one way to fulfilment. It is never too late to find your purpose in life, no matter how old you are or how far you have travelled on a particular route.

The most crucial assignment or responsibility you have is to be conscious of who and what you are; taking the time to figure out what will make you happy and being intentional about pursuing it. Although, like many others, you may always wish (if only you could turn the clock back) you had started out earlier in life, it will still be a great source of joy that you did it anyway, regardless of the timeline. Being content with yourself and what you do is a significant discovery and gift; being still able to do what makes you happy is what truly matters.

I urge you to avert any anxieties you may have inflicted upon yourself or the extraordinary volume of pressure that society may have exacted upon you – demanding that you prove your worth in your younger years. Making changes at any stage or age is a step in the right direction. Challenge your limits and go for the change you sincerely desire, to make the kind of impact you have always been concerned about. Since you are ultimately responsible for your happiness, it is of significant importance that you begin to develop or change into your true self.

Embracing Purpose in Later Life

There are many inspiring stories of people that have hiked the peak of their purpose in older life. Discovering your purpose later in life doesn't diminish its significance; instead, it amplifies its impact. Let's reflect on the story of Julia Child, the renowned chef and culinary icon who introduced French cuisine to the American public. Julia didn't find her passion for cooking until her late 30s when she moved to Paris with her husband. Enrolling in the Le Cordon Bleu cooking school ignited her culinary journey. Despite being a late bloomer, she dedicated years to mastering the art of French cooking. At the age of 49, she published her first cookbook, eventually hosting popular TV shows that made her a household name.

Grandma Moses, a celebrated folk artist, embarked on her artistic journey in her late 70s. With no formal training in art, she began painting seriously when arthritis made embroidery challenging. Using house paint and canvas boards, her folk art depicting rural life caught the eye of an art collector. This discovery led her to become a celebrated artist, exhibiting her works in galleries, and selling them for significant value.

These stories exemplify that age is not a limitation when it comes to discovering one's purpose. Just like Julia Child and Grandma Moses, anyone can embark on a transformative journey at any stage of life.

The courage to start anew, to pivot, and to align one's life with their true calling holds the potential to reshape destinies, no matter how many years have passed. Whether it's through cooking, painting, writing, or any other pursuit, finding purpose later in life is not just about personal fulfilment but also about leaving an indelible mark on the world.

Their stories serve as inspiring encouragement, reminding us that discovering one's purpose isn't confined to youth; it's an ever-unfolding journey that can begin afresh at any moment, guiding us toward a life that resonates with passion, joy, and profound significance. Your aspirations, dreams, and potential have no expiration date.

Inspirational Journeys to New Beginnings Abraham – Fruitfulness in Old Age

Against the waning light of his years, Biblical Abraham stands as a figure of perseverance and hope. Age had draped him in

The Importance of Starting Afresh

wisdom, yet the promise of his purpose, to become a father of many nations, remained an unfulfilled whisper from the Creator.

It was amidst this backdrop of fading chances that Abraham's story teaches us the most profound lesson: Starting afresh on the right path is not merely a step; it is the greatest leap toward the fulfilment of one's purpose.

"Abraham, look at the stars," said the voice that had guided him to leave behind everything familiar, "so shall your offspring be." It was a call to look beyond the present, to envision a future as boundless as the night sky. And in that moment, Abraham chose to embrace a dawn yet unseen, to start anew with the belief that it is never too late to align with one's true calling.

To start afresh, as Abraham did, is to acknowledge that the past need not dictate the future. It is to allow oneself to be reborn from the ashes of yesterday's expectations into the vibrant possibility of today. In Abraham's journey, we find the courage to shake off the dust of old roads and venture into new territories of self-discovery and purpose.

> *In the art of beginning anew, we find the truest progress, the kind that leads us closer to the fulfilment of our own promised lands.*

Let us hold fast to the notion that the seeds we plant today in the soil of renewal may one day blossom into legacies as numerous and luminous as the stars that guided Abraham. In the art of beginning anew, we find the truest progress, the kind that leads us closer to the fulfilment of our own promised lands.

Let me share a few more inspirational stories of people who took a journey to start afresh.

Vera Wang - A Leap into Design

In the realm of fashion, few stories resonate with the power of reinvention quite like that of Vera Wang. Before her foray into the world of bridal couture, Wang's aspirations were rooted in the ice rinks where she dreamed of Olympic glory. Following a pivot from figure skating, she entrenched herself in the fashion industry, climbing the ranks to become a senior fashion editor at Vogue. However, it was a personal quest for the perfect wedding gown that catalysed her venture into the bridal fashion industry.

Approaching her 40th birthday, Wang grappled with the realisation that the ideal wedding dress eluded her grasp. It was this very search that illuminated a gap in the market. With a blend of hesitation and audacity, Wang pondered over her father's proposal to design her own dress, an opportunity that eventually burgeoned into a business idea.

Despite the creeping doubts shadowing her thoughts – "Is it too late for me?" – Vera chose to challenge the status quo. With a combination of her father's support and her refined aesthetic sensibility, she embarked on a journey to revolutionise bridal wear. This leap of faith was not merely about changing careers; it was about embracing the unknown at a stage where many might balk at the prospect of starting anew.

Today, Vera Wang's name is synonymous with elegance and innovation in bridal fashion. Her story stands as a beacon for those daunted by the idea of late-life ventures, proving that age is but a number and that the pursuit of passion knows no expiry.

Kweisi Mfume: Resilience and Transformation

Life's most profound lessons often emerge from the depths of adversity. For Kweisi Mfume, the harsh realities of life came crashing down early. The passing of his mother when he was just 16 years old marked the beginning of a tumultuous period. Bereft of guidance, Mfume found himself adrift, struggling with the responsibilities of fatherhood and the absence of a high school diploma, as he welcomed five children into the world before his

This Space; Your Place

20th birthday.

Yet, within the crucible of these trials, the seeds of change were sown. It was in the silence of reflection, as he trod the challenging path of a young father, that Mfume's moment of clarity dawned. With the resolve to redefine his life narrative, he embraced the transformative power of education. His journey back to academic pursuit was not merely a return to structured learning but a passionate quest for a brighter future.

Enrolling in community college marked the turning point. Mfume's dedication and tenacity saw him ascend through academic ranks, culminating in a triumphant graduation from the prestigious Johns Hopkins University. This achievement was not a final destination but the opening of a new chapter.

Mfume's commitment to growth and service propelled him into the political arena, where he became a beacon of hope and progress. His election to the Baltimore City Council was a testament to his leadership and vision. It was a journey that continued through the hallowed halls of Congress and led to the pinnacle of advocacy as the president of the NAACP (National Association for the Advancement of Coloured People).

Kweisi Mfume's story is a powerful reminder that our

beginnings do not dictate our endings. It speaks to the heart of every individual who has faced setbacks and challenges. His life is an inspiring narrative that shows us that with determination and a willingness to turn one's life around, every moment of despair can be transformed into a step towards a significant and impactful existence.

Reflections and Action Points

Embark on an introspective journey. In this section, 'Reflections and Action Points,' I invite you to pause and go deeper into your thoughts. These thought-provoking questions are not just words on a page but invitations to explore the corridors of your soul, to assess where you stand, and to envision where you aim to be.

Take a moment to ponder, to challenge the status quo, and to consider the path that aligns most with your aspirations. These queries are stepping stones towards meaningful action, guiding you to carve *your place* toward purpose and fulfilment in *this space*. Let's begin this transformative journey together.

1. What are the top three things you've always wanted to accomplish, yet somehow postponed or abandoned? How can

you rekindle these aspirations starting today?

_____

_____

_____

2. Reflecting on your past experiences, which moments made you feel the most fulfilled or alive? How can you integrate more of these moments into your daily life to align better with your purpose?

_____

_____

_____

3. What dreams have you shelved due to fear or uncertainty, and how might embracing discomfort help reignite their pursuit?

_____

_____

_____

_____

4. Think about a time when you felt most disconnected from your true self. What changes or decisions can you make to reconnect with your authentic purpose?

_____

_____

_____

5. If there were no limitations or fears holding you back, what bold step towards your purpose would you take right now?

_____

_____

_____

6. Consider your daily routine. How much of your time is spent on activities that truly resonate with your passions and align with your purpose? What adjustments can you make to prioritise these activities?

_____

_____

_____

7. Reflect on your most significant life goals. What is the first step you can take today to progress toward one of these goals?

_____

_____

_____

_____

Call to Action

Your journey towards discovering *your place* in *this space* commences now. Embrace this moment as the catalyst for transformation. Take that first step today, knowing that within it lies the seed for profound change.

Actionable Steps:

1. **Reflect and Journal**: Allocate daily time for introspection. Keep a journal to record musings, dreams, and flashes of inspiration.

2. **Spotlight Passions and Strengths**: Compile a list of pursuits or interests that genuinely spark joy. Assess your

strengths and abilities that harmonise with these passions.

3. **Seek Mentorship and Coaching**: Engage in dialogues with trusted confidants, mentors, or therapists. Absorb their insights into your strengths and the uniqueness you bring.

4. **Experiment New Paths**: Initiate small trials to explore fresh interests or revisit old passions. Enrol in courses, join communities, or offer your time to causes that captivate your curiosity.

5. **Set Goals and Make Steps**: Outline short-term and long-term objectives based on your reflections. Execute actionable steps towards these goals, no matter their seeming insignificance.

Remember, every stride you take towards your purpose inches you closer to a life brimming with fulfilment. Embrace uncertainty with fortitude. Your path is distinctive, and its commencement is a testament that it's never too late to inscribe your unique story.

Starting Afresh in *This Space*

In this vast space, there are moments when we feel lost, entangled in the illusion of failure, and adrift in the absence of purpose. It is in these profound valleys of our existence that the voices of self-doubt echo relentlessly, drowning out the potential for a fresh beginning.

Yet, let me impart a truth that transcends the confines of these moments: the measure of our lives is not defined by the setbacks we encounter. Rather, it is in the courage to rise after each fall that we uncover the raw essence of resilience. For when the heart is heavy with the weight of perceived failure, it is then that the spirit calls for renewal.

Starting afresh isn't an act reserved for the fortunate few who've never tasted the bitter cup of defeat. No, it's an invitation extended to every soul weary from the burden of unfulfilled dreams and life's unexpected detours. There is nothing wrong about starting anew and reinventing yourself. You can begin again from where you are. Most great people who have accomplished exceptional things have done so primarily by making a comeback from exceptional crunches.

When purpose feels elusive, and the specter of failure looms large, it's crucial to acknowledge that our setbacks aren't tombstones; they're mere commas in the grand narrative of our lives. Your story is not confined to a chapter of missteps or unmet

The Importance of Starting Afresh

expectations. Instead, it's an evolving saga, waiting for the ink of resilience to script a fresh page.

Embrace the notion that within the thoughts, of your perceived failures, lies the ideas for your greatest victories. The dormant dreams within you yearn for a resurrection, longing to bloom despite the wintry frost of discouragement.

Purpose isn't a distant mirage; it's the spark that flickers in the depths of your being, awaiting the gentle breath of inspiration to ignite a roaring fire. Even when the embers seem dim, stoke the flame of hope, for therein lies the light guiding you towards a new dawn.

So, if you find yourself standing within the wreckage of shattered dreams, take solace in this truth: your story isn't over. The divine architect of destinies invites you to lay the foundation of a fresh beginning, fashioning a narrative that transcends the limitations of past disappointments.

As you stand at this crossroads, let the lessons of yesterday be the stepping stones towards a purposeful tomorrow. For in the sanctuary of new beginnings lies the profound beauty of embracing the unknown and birthing a life replete with purpose, resilience, and unbridled possibilities.

This Space; Your Place

As you stand at the precipice of this transformative journey, poised to embark on the path towards *your place* in *this space*, remember this: time and change are critically imminent. They are constant, unwavering forces that shape the very essence of your existence. Therefore, invest in yourself and in time itself, for it is the currency through which change weaves its thread in your life.

Change, that unstoppable tide, sweeps through the corridors of our existence, guiding us through seasons of growth and evolution. Embrace it, for it is in embracing change that we discover the hidden treasures within us – those gems of resilience, adaptability, and uncharted potential.

Do not squander the precious currency of time by dwelling amidst the debris of past sorrows. Instead, fix your gaze steadfastly on the horizon of possibilities. Believe in the divine hand that orchestrates *this space*, guiding your steps even when the path seems obscure. But, above all, believe in yourself – the reservoir of strength and resilience waiting to be unfurled.

> *Do not squander the precious currency of time by dwelling amidst the debris of past sorrows.*

Guard your heart against the noise of doubters, those who seek to trivialise or ridicule your journey. You are not merely a

The Importance of Starting Afresh

traveller; you are a pilgrim on a life changing quest. Your end is not defined by the scars of yesterday but by the unwritten chapters waiting to be penned by your spirit's indomitable courage.

You cannot forge a brighter tomorrow if you linger too long in the shadows of yesterday. Your tomorrow is adorned with the radiance of promise and the glow of untapped potential.

As you conclude this book and turn the page to the next phase of your life, carry with you the unshakeable belief that within the chasms of change and the eternal flow of time, lies the promise of *your place* in *this space*.

The world is waiting on you – not just any version of you, but the best version of you. They may be waiting for the solutions you will provide, the words you will speak, the art you will create, or the leadership you will exhibit. Their waiting is not passive; it is filled with expectation and hope.

What you are not willing to die for, you cannot truly live for. Your purpose is worth fighting for – so fight the good fight for *your place* in *this space*. Do not let them wait in vain. Your action, your decision to move forward, can be the turning point. So please, with urgency and purpose, get up, dress up, and show up. The world awaits the story only you can tell, the journey only you can embark on, and the legacy only you can leave.

It's your time to take *Your Place in This Space!*

Chapter 11 Highlights

1. Age should never deter one from pursuing new goals or redefining life's direction. Starting anew at any moment is pivotal for aligning with one's true purpose.
2. You will deeply regret passing away without having fulfilled your true calling or completing what you were meant to do.
3. No matter your past, starting afresh with the belief in your potential is the cornerstone of fulfilling your life's purpose.
4. There is profound joy and satisfaction in discovering and aligning with your right path, which leads to true happiness and impact.

Invitation to Connect

Your journey towards discovering your purpose and embracing a new chapter in your life has just begun. I invite you to be an active part of this transformative experience.

Get in Touch: Connect with me to share your thoughts, reflections, and personal discoveries inspired by *This Space; Your Place*. Your insights could be a guiding light for others on a similar path. Whether you've had moments of epiphany, challenges you wish to discuss, or success stories to inspire, I'm eager to hear from you.

Feel free to reach out on Social Media or visit our website www.skillsmindset.com

Your unique journey matters, and your voice is an invaluable addition to our collective conversation.

Listen to my Podcast: In the spirit of growth and mutual support, consider subscribing to our weekly podcast on all major platforms - The SkillsMindset Podcast which brings you more than just information and knowledge. It's there to help you discover yourself and maximise your potential through effective use of your talent, skillset, and experience. It is about you developing and evolving into a future that is visible, achievable and rewarding.

Remember, your participation enriches not only your journey but also that of others seeking their path to fulfilment. Let's create a vibrant, nurturing space where our collective pursuit of purpose flourishes.

Thank You for Reading My Book!

Your support means the world to me. I deeply value your feedback and am genuinely interested in hearing your thoughts.

Your input will significantly contribute to enhancing my future literary works.

Would you kindly spare a moment to share your insights by leaving a review on Amazon? Your feedback will help me understand your thoughts on the book better.

Thank you immensely for your time and consideration.

Warm regards, Gbenga Lawal

About The Author

Dr. Gbenga Lawal is a transformational leader and solutions consultant. His work has provided crucial interventions to individuals and organisations, and he continues to make a meaningful impact. With an academic background focused on guiding many towards successful careers, he has transformed into a global champion of personal and corporate growth and development. Gbenga firmly believes that the future starts today and that every individual possesses the ability to achieve desired outcomes. These values have not only shaped his own personal transformation but also guide his work as a consultant, facilitator of learning and change, businessman, and philanthropist.

Furthermore, Gbenga is a Management and Leadership Fellow of the Chartered Institute of Management and Leadership (FCIML) in Delaware, United States. He is also a facilitator of the Beyond Success Programme by John C Maxwell. Additionally, he holds the esteemed title of Fellow of the Royal Society for Arts, Manufactures and Commerce (FRSA) in the United Kingdom and is a member of the United Nations Association (UNA-UK).

In his professional capacity, Gbenga serves as the CEO and Director at Skillsmindset Limited, Potters Property Holdings Limited, and Relief Efforts Foundation. He is also a member of the Trust Board at the Thurrock African Group (TAG) in the United Kingdom.

www.ingramcontent.com/pod-product-compliance
Lightning Source LLC
Chambersburg PA
CBHW030332230426
43661CB00032B/1388/J